simple
soft furnishings

KATRIN CARGILL

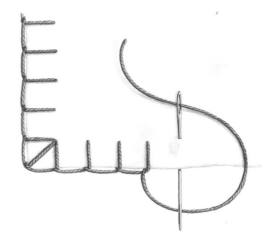

simple

KATRIN CARGILL

soft furnishings

50 stylish home sewing projects
to transform your home

photography by David Montgomery

QUADRILLE

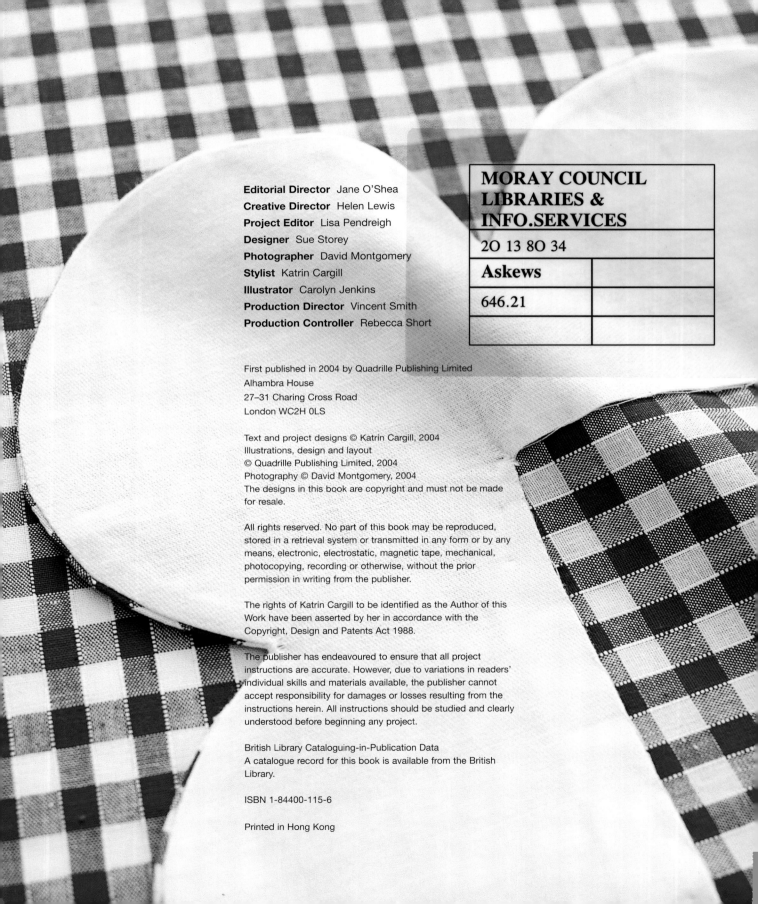

Editorial Director Jane O'Shea
Creative Director Helen Lewis
Project Editor Lisa Pendreigh
Designer Sue Storey
Photographer David Montgomery
Stylist Katrin Cargill
Illustrator Carolyn Jenkins
Production Director Vincent Smith
Production Controller Rebecca Short

First published in 2004 by Quadrille Publishing Limited
Alhambra House
27–31 Charing Cross Road
London WC2H 0LS

British Library Cataloguing-in-Publication Data
A catalogue record for this book is available from the British
Library.

ISBN 1-84400-115-6

Printed in Hong Kong

contents

introduction

The busier our lives and the less secure the outside world becomes, the more we want to cocoon ourselves in our homes. As a result, the home furnishings industry has boomed over the last few decades.. From furniture superstores to fancy fabric houses, from the plethora interiors books and magazines, it's hard not be conscious of our home environment and want our houses to resemble the glossy images that bombard us. Achieving the style you are striving for, be it farmhouse country or slick city chic, doesn't comes easily to most people. You are left with the choice of either trying your own hand at cobbling together a 'look' or finding and employing an interior designer at considerable expense. So, it is a good thing to arm yourself with as much information and knowledge as possible: clip photographs from magazines to create a file of favourite looks, collect paint and fabric samples that you like and, before you know it, you will have honed down your personal style to something unique to you.

Having grown up a rather nomadic child; living everywhere from Tunisia to America, via Scandinavia and England, my immediate home surroundings have always been very important to me. Getting nested in a new home meant fixing up my bedroom as a matter of urgency. Usually it meant a coat of paint in one of the colours of the moment (during my teenages years is was a groovy luminous orange) and, if I was lucky, a new pair of curtains, a bedspread and some cushions. Gradually I developed a colour palette of my own and, as I travel and see new colour combinations and styles, so my look develops and changes.

The next step is implementing these ideas in your home. You can transform a room dramatically with a few new soft furnishings. Because the projects in this book are easy to make, you won't be stuck with them forever; when styles and colours change, so can your home with a few quick and easy sewing ideas. Simple Soft Furnishings is divided into five sections: cushions, including everything from a basic bed bolster to a gathered round plump cushion; curtains and blinds,

from a simple no-sew curtain to a more sophisticated contrast-lined roman blind; bedlinens, filled with fun bedspread ideas; tablelinens, which includes cute gingham napkins with velvet edging; seating, which is filled with ideas from a simple loose cover to a fitted dining chair cover with box pleats. Each chapter is devoted to ideas that can take mere moments, like the Lace-edged Coverlet on page 90, or more personal projects, which involve some planning and a bit of hand stitching, like the Cot Quilt with Embroidered Initial on page 110.

I have deliberately used strong colours throughout to create graphic images, so you may want to adapt the colours of a project to suit your own palette. One of the hardest things to choose is fabric. Most people are just bamboozled by the choice and prints and plains, but if you go back to your basic file of favourite looks, you will probably find you have a small range of fabrics, colours and textures that you are really drawn to, so stick with those. Remember to be practical when choosing fabric: neither a loose cover for a sofa made from a heavy unwashable cloth nor dark, dye-laden fabric for a bedding or table project make much sense. If in doubt, pre-wash a sample of the fabric to see how it reacts. Because so many of these projects are simple, attention to detail is paramount. Combining colours is important and the details like trimmings, beadings, and ribbons make the difference between a really great stylish product and a more mediocre one.

This book has been designed to inspire you not only to transform your home, but principally to get you sewing. Many of the projects can be made by simple hand stitching, but of course a sewing machine will make very light work of it. It really does make sense to be as well equipped for the job as possible; when cooking, the basic pans and utensils make tasks so much easier, and so it is with sewing. A good sewing machine will stay with you for life. A sturdy work surface for cutting fabric is also useful and good working light is essential. Don't scrimp on scissors, pins, tape measure or cotton thread as it will only compromise your efforts.

Happy sewing!

cushions

simple cushion

This basic cushion cover uses a simple stitched envelope opening, so you don't need to wrestle with any tricky fastenings. The cushion pad slips neatly into the opening at the back, making it convenient for laundering.

Materials

Fabric, such as lightweight cotton or linen

Sewing thread

Ready-made monogram or embroidery cotton

Cushion pad

1 For the front panel, cut a piece of fabric to the size of the cushion pad adding 2cm seam allowance all the way around. For the back panels, cut a piece of fabric the same length but half the width of the cushion pad plus 3cm and adding 2cm seam allowance on the other three sides. Cut another piece of fabric half the width of the cushion pad plus 12cm to the width and adding 2cm seam allowance on the other three sides.

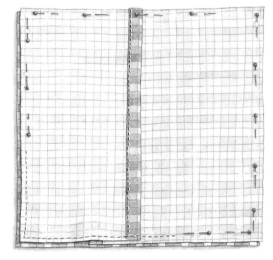

step 3

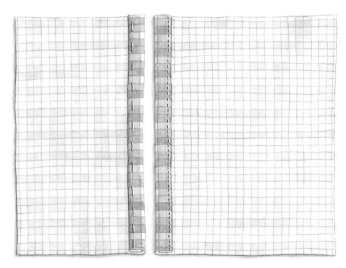

step 2

2 Lay the two back panels right sides down and turn in a double 1cm hem on one short side of each. Pin, tack and then stitch. Press.

3 If using a ready-made monogram, apply it to the front panel. With right sides together, lay the two back panels over the front panel with raw sides edge to edge so that the two seamed edges overlap by 9cm. Pin or tack together 1cm from edges. Stitch. Turn right side out. Press. If required, hand sew a monogram using embroidery cotton to the front of the cushion cover. Insert the cushion pad.

adding a monogram

Sometimes it is possible to find old ready-made monograms in antiques markets, which can be hand sewn onto cushion covers. Old linens often yield monograms that can be cut out as patches and appliquéd to the front of cushion covers, either by hand, using embroidery thread and blanket stitch, or with an overlocker on the machine. Cut around the monogram with sharp scissors, turn under on all sides, press and attach to the front of the cover. It is best to do this before sewing the cushion pieces together in step 2. Hand embroidering a monogram is also special; use embroidery thread and work it in cross stitch or back stitch.

trimmed cushion

Be it piping cord, rickrack, fringing or flat piping, incorporating a trimming into the edges of a cushion cover always uses the same technique: they all sandwich and secure the trimming between the front and back panels of the cushion cover.

Materials

As for Simple Cushion (see page 12)

Rickrack, piping or other trimming

Cushion pad

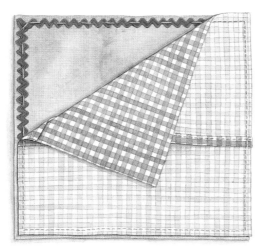

incorporating trimmings

Trimmings without selvedges, such as rope borders, velvet ribbons or beads, can also be used; these need to be applied either to the front panel after it has been cut out and before joining it with the back, or sewn on once the cushion has been stitched together.

trimming a cushion with rickrack

Make the front and back panels as shown in steps 1 and 2 of the Simple Cushion (see page 12). If preferred, use different fabrics for the front and back panels. With the front panel right side up, lay the rickrack trimming around the edges of the fabric so that the centre of its width is 1cm from the raw edges. Pin in place. Tack along the centre of the rickrack. With right sides together, lay the two back panels over the front panel with raw sides edge to edge so that the two seamed edges overlap, as shown in step 3 of the Simple Cushion (see page 12). Pin or tack together 1cm from edges. Stitch very carefully along this line so it follows the centre of the rickrack. Turn right side out. Press. Insert the cushion pad.

trimming a cushion with piping

When using piping to trim a cushion, lay the piping around the edges of the front panel so the raw sides of the panel and the selvedge of the piping are edge to edge and the piped side lies 1cm inside the cushion edge. With right sides together, lay the two back panels over the front panel with raw sides edge to edge so that the two seamed edges overlap, as shown in step 3 of the Simple Cushion (see page 12). Pin or tack together 1cm from edges. Stitch carefully along this line so it is as close as possible to the piped edge. Turn right side out. Press. Insert the cushion pad.

ruffle-edged cushion

One of the most speedy and effective ways of freshening up a tired-looking room is to add some new cushions. There is always a huge selection available in the stores, but when you realise how easy it is to make your own, you will be able to transform a room in a weekend. And what is more refreshing fabric than the humble cotton ticking?

ruffle-edged cushion

Materials

Fabric, such as
cotton ticking

Sewing thread

Zip that is 10cm
shorter than the width
of the cushion pad

Cushion pad

Add a softly gathered ruffle to a plain cushion cover and the look is as comfortable in a country setting as in a minimal interior. Easy-to-follow instructions for putting in a zip are given here to add you a useful sewing skill to a repertoire.

1 For the front panel, cut a piece of fabric to the size of the cushion pad adding 2cm seam allowance all the way around. For the back panels, cut two pieces of fabric the same length but half the width of the cushion pad adding 2cm seam allowance all the way around. For a 6.5cm-deep ruffle, cut a strip of fabric $2^1/_2$ times the perimeter of the cushion pad by 17cm. If necessary, join pieces of fabric together to achieve the required length.

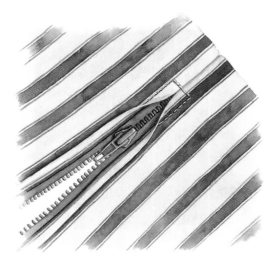

step 3

step 2

2 For the back panel, place the two back panels right sides together and stitch 5cm in from each outside edge with a 2cm seam allowance. Open out the seams and press along both stitched and unstitched sections.

3 Turn the back panel right side up and lay the closed zip right side up underneath the opening, between the two seams, ensuring the fabric meets over the middle of the zip. Pin and tack the zip in place. Slipstitch the opening along the pressed edges so they meet. Topstitch down one side, across the end and up the other side of the zip using a zipper foot if machining. Remove the slipstitches. Open the zip before you continue.

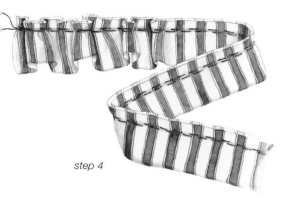

step 4

4 For the ruffle, stitch together the two short ends leaving a 2cm seam allowance to make a continuous band. Open out the seam and press. Fold the sewn band in half widthwise with the right side out and press. Hand sew a double row of running stitches 2cm from the open edge. Pull the threads to form even gathers until the band is the same size as the perimeter of the cushion pad.

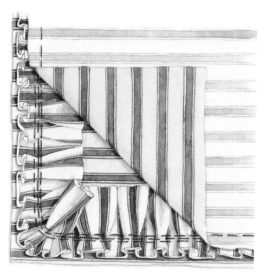

step 5

5 With the front panel right side up, lay the gathered ruffle around the perimeter of the front panel so that the raw edges are edge to edge. Pin and tack the ruffle 2cm from the outside edge. Place the back panel over the top, right side down. Pin and tack together 2cm from edges. Stitch carefully around all four sides just inside this line so that the gathering stitches of the ruffle are not visible. At each corner, work the stitches in a curve rather than a right angle. Trim the edges and clip the corners. Turn right side out through the zip opening. Press. Insert the cushion pad.

scallop-edged cushion

The elegant curves of a scalloped flap add sophistication to household cotton ticking, as they would to almost any other fabric. The corners of the scallops are mitred to form a border for the cushion.

1 Make the front and back panels with a zip opening as shown in steps 1, 2 and 3 of the Frilled-edge Cushion (see page 18). For the scalloped edge, cut four strips of fabric to the width of the cushion pad adding 2.5cm seam allowance, by 7.5cm plus 2.5cm seam allowance. Cut a further four strips of fabric to the length of the cushion pad plus 2.5cm seam allowance by 7.5cm plus 2.5cm seam allowance.

2 For the scalloped edge, lay one long strip right side up. Place a short strip on top right side down, aligning with one corner. Fold then press the corner at a 45-degree angle. Pin and tack along the

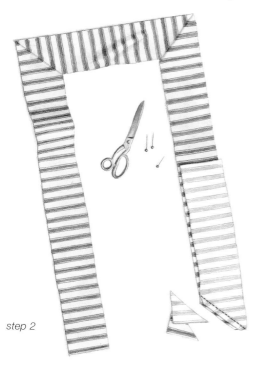

step 2

fold. Stitch. Trim the excess fabric to a 1cm seam allowance. Repeat this for the remaining three corners until you have a rectangular frame. Open out all the corner seams and press. Make a second frame in the same way.

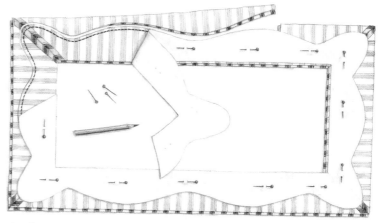

step 3

3 Lay the two frames together right sides facing. Using a paper template, draw the outer edge of the scallop shapes onto the wrong side of the top frame. Remove template. Pin and tack. Stitch all around the outline. Trim the excess fabric to a 1cm seam allowance and snip the curves. Turn right side out. Follow step 5 for Frilled-edge Cushion to finish.

Materials

Fabric, such as cotton ticking

Sewing thread

Zip that is 10cm shorter than the width of the cushion pad

Paper template for scallop shape

Cushion pad

bolster with silk ties

Bolsters serve all sorts of practical and decorative purposes. Awkward angular gaps on sofas, bed ends and day beds can be visually minimised by a plump bolster. Introduce rich colour, texture or pattern into a room with a bolster cover to add a chic accent.

bolster with silk ties

The contrast of turquoise cotton toile de Jouy fabric and the gorgeous iridescent emerald green silk ties on this bolster make a strong, stylish statement. The simple bolster cover is quick and easy to make and can be made from almost any fabric.

1 Cut a piece of fabric to the circumference of the bolster pad adding 2cm seam allowance by the length of the bolster plus twice the required overhang (approximately 40cm here). If the fabric is too narrow, join extra pieces to either end. Fold in half the length of each overhang and press. Stitch 1cm from the folded-in edge.

2 Fold fabric in half lengthwise with right sides together. Pin and tack. Stitch 2cm from the edge. Open out seams and press.

steps 1 and 2

Materials

Fabric, such as medium-weight cotton

Sewing thread

Fabric for making ties, such as silk

Bolster inner/pad

3 To make the tie, cut a piece of silk 50cm wide by 100cm long and fold in half lengthwise. Press. Use a ruler to draw a line at a 45-degree angle on both ends and snip off the excess triangles of silk. Tack the long open side and one short end, 1cm from the raw edges, and stitch. Turn right side out and fold in the raw edges of the open end. Use small, neat slip stitches to close the opening. Press.

step 3

alternative bolster ties

As an alternative to the silk ties, use contrasting velvet ribbon and little gingham roses for a more decorative effect. Scour flea markets for old ribbon and scraps of antique textiles to contrast a modern fabric. To make the gingham rose, follow the instructions for the rosette on page 28.

gathered round cushion

Pretty and pert, round cushions add a touch of couture to any room. Sometimes a space calls for something just that little bit more special than the ubiquitous square padded pillow, and this cushion with circular pleats and a decorative rosette certainly looks unique.

gathered round cushion

Unless you are a very experienced sewer, this cover is easiest to make from a sturdy, tightly woven yet thin fabric as the pleats won't slip away. The opening at the back is a simple flap, though you could as easily insert a zip.

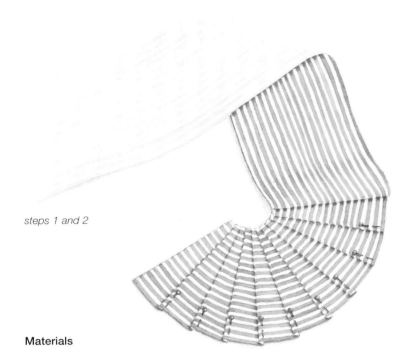

steps 1 and 2

open ends together to hide the raw edges. Gather the pleats around the inner edge to close the centre gap. Secure with tacking stitches. Stitch the seam to close the raw edges. Stitch the outer circumference 2cm from the edge.

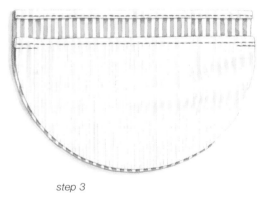

step 3

Materials

Fabric, such as a tightly woven, crisp cotton

Sewing thread

Circular box cushion pad

1 For the front panel, cut a length of fabric one and a two thirds times the circumference of the cushion pad by the radius of the cushion pad plus 2cm seam allowance all the way around. If necessary, join pieces of fabric together to achieve the required length.

2 Fold in and pin pleats around the circle so that around the outer edge they are approximately 5cm wide with a tuck under of one third that width. Secure with tacking stitches. Pin and tack the two

3 For the back panel, draw and cut a semicircle the diameter of the cushion pad plus 2cm seam allowance plus 3.75cm on the straight side. Cut another semicircle with 2cm seam allowance plus 10cm on the straight side. Turn under 1.25cm on both straight sides. Press and stitch. With right sides up, line up the semicircles to form a circle and pin them together. Stitch 5cm in from both outside edges along the straight side of the shorter piece with a 2cm seam allowance. Open out the seams and press along both stitched and unstitched sections. Make two buttonholes along the straight side of the shorter piece either by hand (see page 37) or by machine.

step 4

4 For the side panel, cut a length of fabric twice the circumference of the cushion pad by the width of the pad plus 2cm seam allowance all the way around. Fold in and pin pleats approximately 5cm wide with a tuck under of about one third along the whole length. Check pleated side panel fits the circumference of front panel and adjust if necessary. Secure pleats with tacking stitches. Stitch along both sides of the panel, about 1.25cm in from the raw edges. With right sides together, stitch short ends together.

step 6

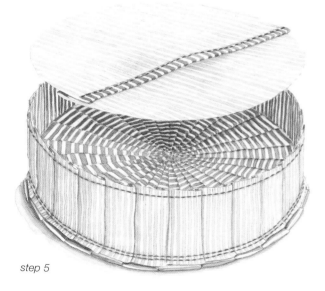

step 5

6 For the rosette, cut four or five circles in graduated sizes, with the largest one big enough to cover all the gathered stitches at the centre of the front panel. Sew through the centre of each circle, gathering a small amount of fabric to make one or two small overlaps in each. Sew through all the circles to join them through their centres. Using tacking stitches, sew the bottom circles to the front panel to secure the rosette.

5 To assemble the cushion, place the pleated front and side panels with right sides together. Pin and tack. Stitch with 2cm seam allowance. Repeat to attach back to side panel. Turn right side out. Press. Sew on buttons to line up with each buttonhole. Insert cushion pad.

box floor cushion

This chunky floor cushion is made from a really strong, robust fabric and a good quality utilitarian linen tea towel. The thick piping gives the cushion the feeling of an old-fashioned mattress. It will have you, the children and the dog fighting over it!

box floor cushion

The technique for making this chunky cushion is easy as the thick piping is actually made like any other piping and stitched into the seams of the cushion. The inner filling could also be made using a sturdy block of foam for greater durability.

1 Using the tea towel or a piece of fabric the same size for the top panel and to determine the size of the cushion. Cut a piece of the fabric for the bottom panel to the same size. For the side panel, cut a length of fabric equal to the perimeter of the top by the depth required plus 2.5cm seam allowance all the way around. Join pieces together if necessary. For the piping, cut two pieces of fabric to the same length as the side panel by 7.5cm. Cut two strips of wadding to the same length by 2.5cm.

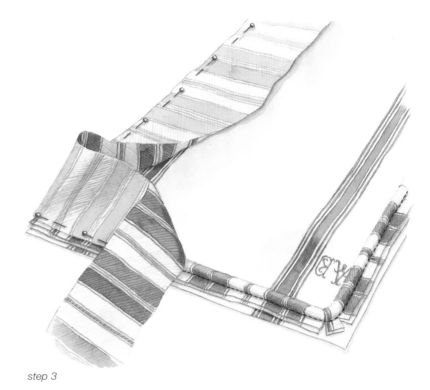

step 3

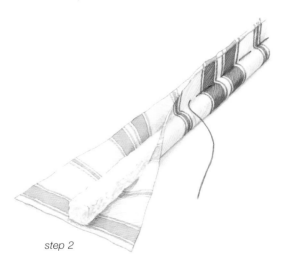

step 2

2 To make the piping, lay the narrow lengths of fabric right side down and place a strip of wadding in the centre of each. Fold fabric in half lengthwise to enclose the wadding, aligning the raw edges. Pin and tack down long edge as close as possible to the wadding. Stitch.

3 With the top panel right side up, lay the piping all the way around the outer edges aligning the raw edges. Pin and tack. Place the side panel all the way around the piped edge of the top panel, again aligning the raw edges and matching any pattern on the side panel to that on the piping. Pin and tack. Stitch as close as possible to the edge of the piping. At each corner, work the stitches in a curve rather than a right angle. Trim the edges and clip the corners.

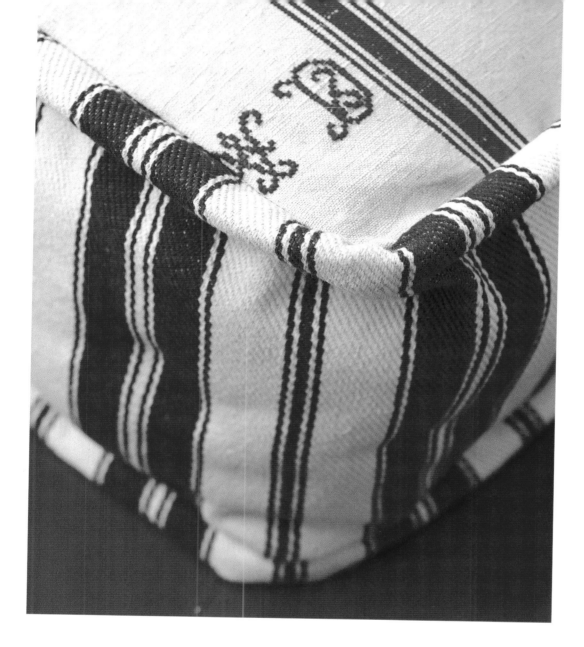

Materials

Fabric panel for top, such as antique linen tea towel

Fabric for bottom, sides and piping, such as sturdy linen

Sewing thread

Wadding for filling and piping

4 Join the bottom panel to the side panel in the same way as for the top, but at one end leave an opening large enough to insert the filling. Cut and stack several layers of wadding a little thicker than required and carefully insert them into the cushion cover.. Close the opening using small, neat slip stitches.

alternative uses

This type of boxy cushion can be used as more than just a floor cushion. The style lends itself particularly well to window seats and benches, especially where a more traditional style is called for. Always use a sturdy fabric like a linen for durability, which might be checked, striped or printed.

buttoned cushion sleeve

Heavy cream linen buttoned over delicate toile de Jouy cotton gives a unique and modern feel to cushions. The linen gives the effect of a loose cover for the cushion. Using antique linen for this idea works beautifully and can even incorporate a monogram.

buttoned cushion sleeve

To make this buttoned cover almost any fabric would be suitable but the rich and heavy feel of the linen adds some weight. If you have a buttonhole facility on your machine, so much the better, but you can also hand stitch buttonholes using a heavy cotton or linen thread and give the cushion a more original look.

Materials

Simple Cushion (see page 12)

Fabric for cover, such as linen

Small amount of fabric to match Simple Cushion, for covered buttons

Sewing thread

Button covering kit, to make 5 buttons

Buttonhole thread

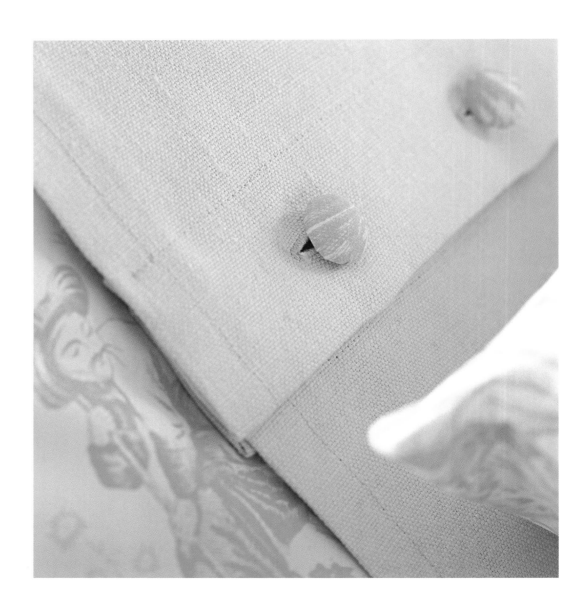

1 Using a soft tape measure, measure around the 'belly' of the Simple Cushion. For the sleeve, cut a piece of fabric 18cm shorter than the length of the Simple Cushion by the 'belly' measurement plus 12.5cm seam allowance. Cut five circles of the Simple Cushion cover fabric for buttons following the kit instructions.

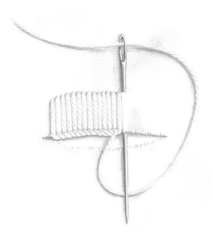

step 3

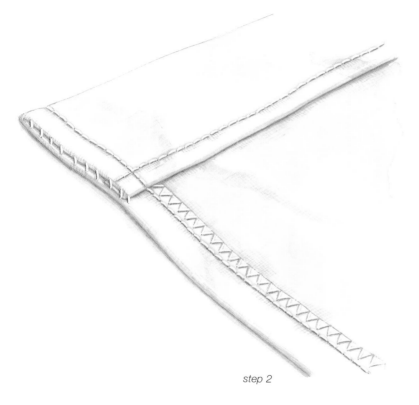

step 2

2 Zigzag stitch along both long sides of the cover to prevent fraying. Fold each side in by 2.5cm and press. Turn and stitch as close as possible to the zigzagged edges. Zigzag stitch both short ends. Fold each side in by 0.5cm and press. Turn in a further 3.75cm and press. Stitch as close as possible to the turned-in edge. Close the four open sides using small neat, slip stitches.

3 To make the buttonholes, measure and mark a line at five evenly spaced points along the centre of the turned-in hem 2cm from the edge. Carefully cut buttonholes along the marked lines, ensuring each is just slightly larger than the diameter of the buttons. Ensure that the button will fit the buttonholes before stitching around the edges of each slit using either the buttonholer on your machine or by hand with buttonhole stitch.
To stitch by hand, secure the thread at the end of the slit furthest away from the edge of the fabric. Work evenly spaced buttonhole stitches to the other end of the slit. Work an uneven number of buttonhole stitches of the same length in a semicircle around the end of the slit. Stitch back along the other side of the slit. Finally, work a row of short buttonhole stitches at right angles to the other stitches and fasten off.

4 Cover all the buttons with the circles of fabric, following the kit instructions. Sew the buttons onto the corresponding side of the cover aligning with the buttonholes. Press. Insert the Simple Cushion and button up the cover.

decorated cushions

Embellish a plain cushion with appliqué work to personalise it. Add touches of colour, or trim it with strips of decorative or antique ribbon. The heavy red linen would also be perfect for embroidering onto – imagine a cross-stitched monogram in a vibrant orange for a modern interpretation of embroidery.

ribbon-decorated cushion

Materials

Fabric, such as
heavyweight linen

Decorative ribbon

Sewing thread

Cushion pad

There are so many wonderful trimmings and ribbons available today, although many of them are very costly. Used sparingly you need very little to make a big impact. Run the ribbon in even stripes or random patterns or mix colours – the idea is to make it your own!

1 For the front panel, cut a piece of fabric to the size of the cushion pad plus 2cm seam allowance all the way around. For the back panel, cut a piece of fabric half the width of the cushion pad plus 3cm on one side and 2cm seam allowances on the other three sides. Cut another piece of fabric half with width of the cushion pad adding 12cm to the width and a further 2cm seam allowance on the other three sides.

step 3

3 For the ties, cut two strips of fabric 45cm long by 5cm wide. Zigzag stitch around all four sides of each tie to prevent fraying. Turn in 1cm on both long ends. Press. Stitch. Turn in 1cm on both short ends. Press and stitch.

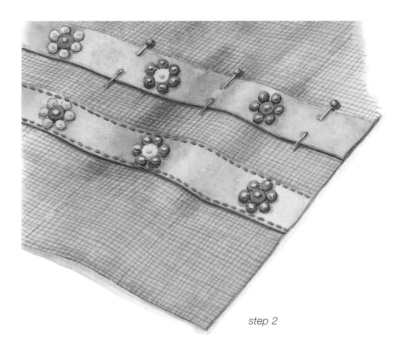

step 2

2 Cut four lengths of decorative ribbon to the same width as the front panel and stitch along both long edges to secure them.

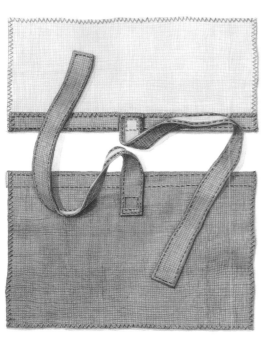

step 4

4 Zigzag stitch around all four sides of the front panel and both back panels. Lay the two back panels right side down. Turn in 2cm on one short side of each. Press. Stitch twice – once near the front fold and once near the zigzagged edge. Take the shorter of the two back panels and with the right side down pin one of the ties in the centre with the end of the tie aligning with the hemmed edge of the panel. Tack, then stitch. Take the wider of the two back pieces and with the right side facing up pin the other tie in the centre with the end 7.5cm inside the hemmed edge of the panel. Tack, then stitch just inside the short ends and extending about 2.5cm on either side of the long ends.

5 With right sides together, lay the two back panels over the front panel with raw sides edge to edge so that the two seamed edges overlap by 9cm. Pin and tack together 2cm from the edges. Stitch. Turn right side out. Press. Insert the cushion pad.

appliqué-decorated cushion

Materials

Fabric, such as
heavyweight linen

Felt in two contrasting
colours

Embroidery cotton in
two contrasting
colours to match felt

Sewing thread

Cushion pad

Appliqué work is a needlecraft skill that has been used for centuries to personalise textiles. With this strong motif and vibrant coloured felt, the traditional detail of handmade French knots looks very contemporary. Felt is a good fabric for appliqué work as it does not fray.

1 Follow all step 1 as given for Ribbon-decorated Cushion.

2 For the appliqué, trace a pattern onto a piece of felt. Carefully cut around the outline. Trace a smaller pattern onto a different colour felt. Cut carefully around the outline. Cut out a small circle of the same colour felt as the largest appliqué pattern piece. Layer, pin and tack all three pieces of felt to the front panel.

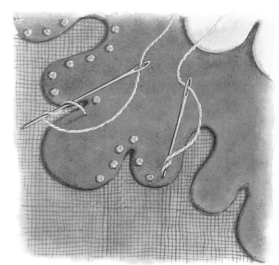

step 3

3 Using contrasting embroidery cotton, work around the outside edge of the largest piece of felt using evenly spaced French knots. Attach the middle and smallest felt pieces in the same way.

4 Proceed as given for Ribbon-decorated Cushion (see page 40).

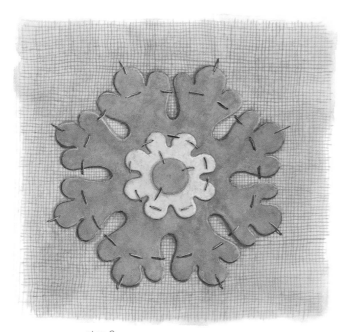

step 2

appliqué work

The great thing about appliqué work is that you can use any design or pattern; make a paper template to try out the size and shape before you cut the fabric. Be inspired by nature, or take the pattern from a piece of china or a colour from another fabric in the room. You can use an overlocker to attach the appliqué to the cushion, simple running stitch or even fusible web; just remember to use a fabric that is tightly woven to stop it looking tattered.

curtains

basic clip-on curtains

For a really quick and easy pair of curtains, it's hard to beat the simplicity of metal curtain clips. There are no handmade headings or curtain tapes to grapple with, all you need to do is hem each curtain all the way around, gather the top into fairly even pleats and attach the clips. Almost any fabric can be used for this method: an antique quilt looks stunning at a window and provides some insulation, too.

basic clip-on curtains

Materials

Fabric, such as
lightweight wool

Sewing thread

Curtain clips

For a natty pair of instant curtains, cheap red felt and metal clips provide a quick makeover for a window. These curtains can be made entirely by hand if you don't have access to a sewing machine; the instructions below are for this method.

1 Cut two drops of fabric to the required length plus 23cm. For the first curtain, turn in both sides 1.25cm, press, then turn in a further 2.5cm, and press. Pin, tack and slip stitch by hand down both sides. Use small slip stitches to close up both turnovers at either end.

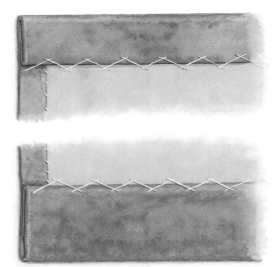

step 2

step 1

2 Turn down the top 2.5cm and press, then turn down a further 5cm and press. Herringbone stitch down by hand. Turn up the bottom 5cm, press and turn up a further 7.5cm and press. Herringbone stitch down by hand and close up the turn-ups both ends with small, neat slip stitches. To hang, put the clips on the pole and gather up small double pleats for each clip, evenly spaced apart. Repeat for second curtain.

Curtain clips come in so many guises now, but the basic principle always remains; a clip incorporates a gather in the fabric to give a draped look.

Top left: Hefty wrought iron clips can hold even heavy fabric.

Top right: New magnetic clips are elegant and practical for lighter materials.

Bottom left: Traditional clips, which can be painted.

Bottom right: Contemporary chrome mini-clips are surprisingly sturdy.

contrast lined curtains

In a bathroom, where light as well as privacy is required , one solution is diaphanous modern lace lined with a thin silk. These layers are sewn together only at the top and are then gathered onto a metal rod with a pocket heading. Light filters through the layers of fabric to give a pretty summery look.

contrast lined curtains

For this type of window treatment it is important to use two very lightweight fabrics, otherwise the gathering for the pocket heading will look bulky and lumpy. It is also advisable to have the pocket fit the rod quite snugly or it won't gather up as shown in the photograph.

1 First measure or calculate the circumference of the curtain rod. To this measurement add 5cm for the heading and pocket plus 1.25cm for the hem (call this measurement A). To this add the drop required from the bottom of the pocket plus 3.75cm for the seam allowance. Cut two drops of this measurement from each of the two fabrics.

2 On all four panels, turn in 1.25cm on each side. Press and turn in a further 1.25cm. Press, then machine down. For the hems turn up 1.25cm and press. Then turn up a further 2.5cm, press and machine down.

step 3

3 Turn down the tops by 0.5cm and press only. Take one of each of the panels and, with the right sides facing down, first turn the inner fabric to the front to measurement A and press. Turn over the outer fabric to the front to cover the back fabric, by the same measurement. Pin and tack.

step 2

Fabric for front, such
as lightweight
cutwork cotton

Fabric for lining in
contrast colour, such
as lightweight silk

Sewing thread

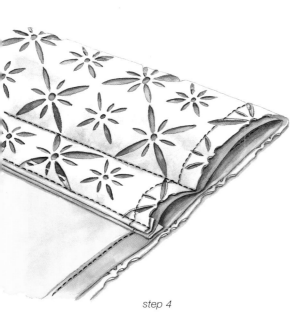

step 4

4 Using tailor's chalk and a metal ruler, draw a line
5cm from the top and another one just above
the folded edge. Machine along these two lines to
form the pocket. Thread the rod into the pocket
and gather up the curtain as required.

alternative fabrics

- -

This laser-cut cotton is a modern-day lace, which instantly portrays a more
contemporary look. Antique lace or a very thin handkerchief linen would also
admit enough light through this type of curtain.

unlined curtains with tape ties

Minimal sewing is required for these smart, tailored curtains. All four sides of the curtain are edged with woven cotton tape, which is also used for the ties that are attached to the wooden curtain rings. The fabric used is a medium-weight linen and cotton mixture that drapes well.

unlined curtains with tape ties

The woven cotton tape not only incorporates the hemming but provides a decorative feature: at the bottom edge of the curtains, an extra band of the tape is sewn horizontally about 25cm from the ground. You could use this technique to create stripes of varying widths.

Materials

Fabric, such as heavyweight linen

Cotton tape

Sewing thread

1 Cut two pieces of the fabric to the drop required plus 2.5cm seam allowance all the way around. For each curtain, cut two lengths of tape the drop of the curtain plus 1.25cm and seven lengths of 76cm each for the ties.

2 With the fabric facing right side up, turn hems to the front 2.5cm down both sides of the curtain. Press. For the decorative band at the bottom of the curtain, cut a length of tape to the width of the curtain and lay it approximately 25cm from the bottom. Tuck the tape into the folded hem at both sides. Trim any excess tape.

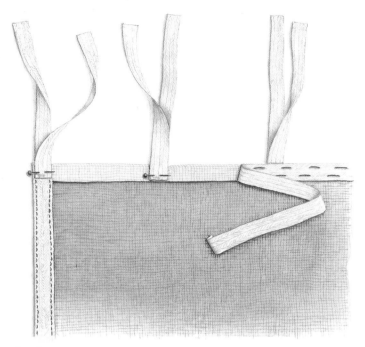

step 4

4 For the bottom, lay a piece of the tape along the bottom edge and turn under 1.25cm on both sides. Pin, tack and machine down along all edges of the tape. For the ties at the top, turn under both short ends 0.5cm on each tie, press and machine down. Fold ties in half and space evenly along the top about 1.25cm from the top of the folded edge.

5 Lay a length of the tape for the top, close to the edge and incorporating the ties. Fold under both ends 0.5cm. Pin, tack and machine down both edges of the tape, and down the short sides.

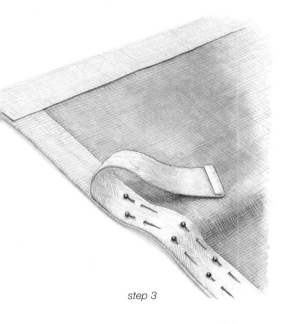

step 3

3 Turn down both the top and bottom of the curtain in the same way and press. For the sides, lay over a length of the tape right to the edge, and turn under the top and bottom of the tape 1.25cm. Pin, tack and machine down both edges of the tape and along the two short ends, to incorporate the hem.

unlined curtains with sewn ties

Make the ties from the same fabric as the curtains, in this case a narrow stripe. The reinforced stitching used to attached the ties – a square box with a criss-cross – can be a decorative feature as it is both strong and attractive. Use a medium- to heavyweight fabric so that the curtains drape well.

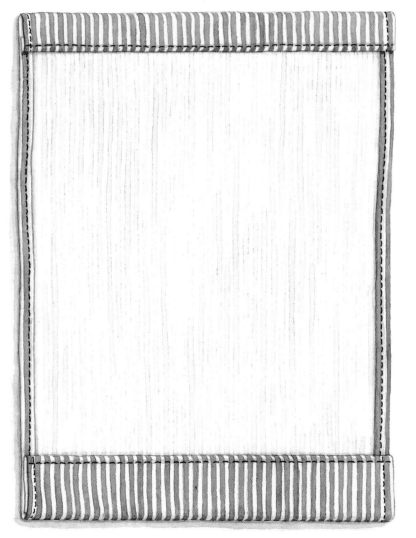

step 2

Materials

Fabric, such as
sturdy, striped cotton

Sewing thread

1 Cut two lengths of the fabric the drop required plus 21.5cm. Cut seven strips of the same fabric, with the stripe running horizontally, 10cm wide by 71cm long.

2 Turn in the sides of each curtain 1.25cm and press. Turn in a further 1.25cm. Press, pin, tack and machine down. Turn down the top 2cm and press. Turn down a further 4.5cm, press, pin, tack and machine down. Turn up the bottom hem 7.5cm, press and turn up a further 7.5cm. Press, pin, tack and machine down.

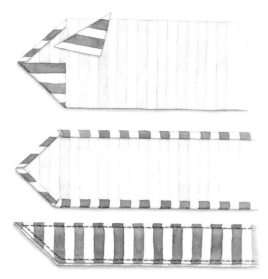

step 3

3 For the ties, fold in each corner at a 45-degree angle. Press and trim back the folds to leave 0.5cm seam allowance. Next fold in 0.5cm down both long edges and press. Fold in half lengthways and press. Pin, tack and machine down round the perimeter of the tie. Repeat for all ties.

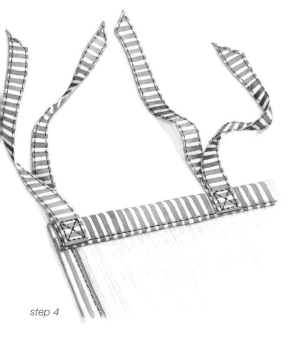

step 4

4 With a curtain right side down, pin one of the ties to each top outside edge and space the rest evenly. Tack, then machine right through to the front, to make the outline of a square, then machine to join opposite corners to form a cross.

lined curtains with tiebacks

These heavily woven linen curtains, with a soft pink checked lining, have hand-sewn headings. The glimpse of a patterned lining behind the plain curtains is an intriguing design detail – the calmness of the plain outer linen belies the pretty, decorative lining. The wide tiebacks are reversible.

lined curtains with tiebacks

Here the lining fabric and the outer fabric are hemmed and sewn edge to edge before being bagged out, making them much simpler than very formal curtains. Once the 'bag' is turned right side out, putting in the pleats is much easier.

Materials

Fabrics for front and back of curtains and tiebacks, preferably same widths

Sewing thread

Buckram 12.5cm deep

Steel hooks

1 Cut three lengths of each fabric to the drop required adding 22cm seam allowance. Fold one length of each of the fabrics in half lengthwise, press and cut in half.

step 2

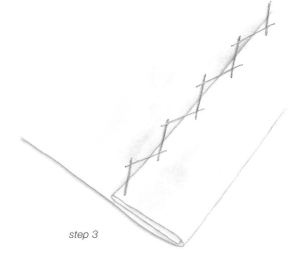

step 3

2 To join widths, lay the full drop right side up with the half width right side down aligning one side. (Always keep the half width to the outer edges of each curtain.) Pin, tack, then machine in 1.25cm from the edges. Snip the selvedges at an angle approximately every 10cm to release any tension. Iron out the seam flat. Make the second curtain in the same way.

3 Turn up the bottom to make a double 10cm hem by first ironing in a crease 20cm up from the lower edge. Open out and fold in a 10cm crease so the raw edge lines up exactly with the first crease. Press. Refold the first crease and herringbone stitch the hem in place. Repeat for both front and back panels of each curtain.

step 4

edge down for 11.5cm. Reverse stitch at the end of each fold to secure. Form the rest of the pleats in the same way. Turn each large pleat into a smaller double pleat by opening out the top edge and pushing in another pleat, creasing the buckram firmly to hold the pleat. Using strong thread, hand stitch across the bottom of the front of each pleat to hold. Attach steel curtain hooks to the back of each pleat.

4 Lay out one of each fabric panels with the right sides facing and cut a length of buckram to the width of the curtain minus 3.75cm. Centre the buckram and aligning it with the top edge, tack in place. Machine the two fabrics and the buckram 2cm down from the top edge. Pin, tack and then machine down both sides leaving 2cm seam allowance. Turn the curtain right side out. Press.

5 For the pleats, work out the finished width required for the curtain and subtract this from the width of the flat curtain. Divide this by the number of pleats you want and mark the centre of each one with a pin at the top of the curtain. Pinch together about 3.75cm either side of each pin and crease the buckram firmly along the fold. Machine the pleat in place from the pin position at the top

step 5

step 6

6 Cut two pieces of each of the fabrics 203cm long by 28cm with all ends at a 45-degree angle. Lay two contrasting pieces right sides together and pin, tack and then machine 0.5cm from the edge, around two long sides, one short side and part of the second short side. Turn right side out and slip stitch the opening. Press.

ruffle-edged curtains

A gorgeous heavy wool needs no lining to provide warmth and insulation on these garden doors. The linen scrim with a silky braid adds a softening decorative touch to the edges. Ordinary heading tape is used for attaching the curtains to the plain metal pole.

ruffle-edged curtains

Materials

Wool or tartan fabric

Sewing thread

Linen scrim

Fan edging trim

5cm-wide curtain
tape

Attaching curtain tape to the heading of a curtain needs to be done methodically: sew one long edge of the tape going from left to right, then reverse this for the other long edge, so the tension is even.

1 Cut two lengths of the fabric to the drop required plus 17cm seam allowances. Cut two lengths of the scrim to one and a half times the drop required by 9cm wide. Cut two lengths of the trim to the drop of the curtain exactly.

2 Lay the fabric right side down and turn in both sides 1.25cm. Pin, tack and then machine the

outer edge. Pin and tack the leading edge, and slipstitch by hand. Turn down the top 2cm, press and herringbone stitch by hand. Lay a length of the curtain tape 0.5cm from the top, and turn under 1.25cm at either end. Pin, tack and machine down along all the edges of the tape.

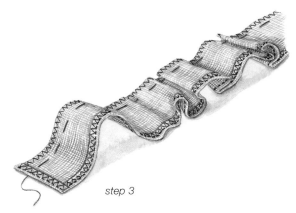

step 3

3 To make the scrim ruffle, zigzag around the perimeter of each strip. Turn in one long edge 0.5cm, press and machine down. Turn down both short edges 0.5cm, press and machine down. Hand sew a running stitch along the unhemmed long edge and gather to the drop required.

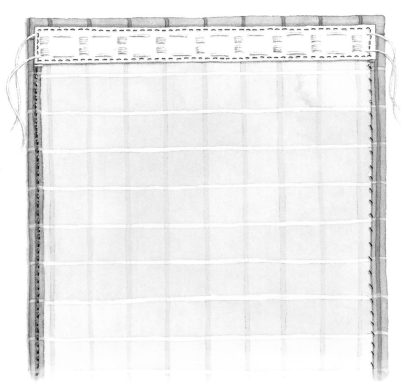

step 2

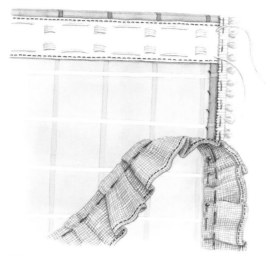

step 4

4 Turn up the bottom of the curtain 7.5cm and
press. Turn up another 7.5cm, press and
herringbone stitch by hand. Lay the curtain right
side down and pin the fan edging along the leading
edge of the curtain so that only the fan part will be
exposed. Pin and tack in place. Lay the gathered
length of scrim over this to cover the selvedge of
the fan edging. Pin, then tack only. Turn the curtain
right side up and machine down the leading edge
to incorporate the fan edging and the scrim.

alternative edgings

Try other ideas for curtain edgings, such as a gathered satin ribbon, glass beading
or ruched fringing. Any of these, or a combination, would work well with wool to
give a contrast of texture and exclude the light.

semi-sheer curtain panels

Cool, calm and collected, this window treatment serves many purposes. The swing arm pole, or portiere rod, lets you control the opening. The sheer upper panels allow light to flood in yet afford privacy, while the opaque lower panels add texture and colour. This is a modern take on window treatment, using a minimal amount of fabric.

semi-sheer curtain panels

Materials

Sheer fabric

Heavier linen

Sewing thread

Because the curtain will be seen from both the front and back when the portiere rods are opened, the fabrics are joined using a French seam – an invisible seam that shows no raw edges.

1 Cut two pieces of the sheer fabric to the drop required plus 7.75cm for seam allowances and the pocket heading by the width required plus 2cm for each side hem. Cut two pieces of the heavier linen to the drop required plus 4.5cm for seam allowances by the width required plus 2cm for each side hem.

Pin, tack and machine 1cm from the edge, securing the ends of the seam by backstitching with the machine. Trim back the seam allowance to 0.5cm. Turn the fabric right sides together and press so that the machined line is right at the edge. Tack, then machine 1cm from the edge. Open out and press the seam to one side.

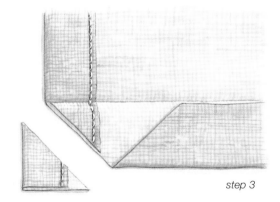

step 3

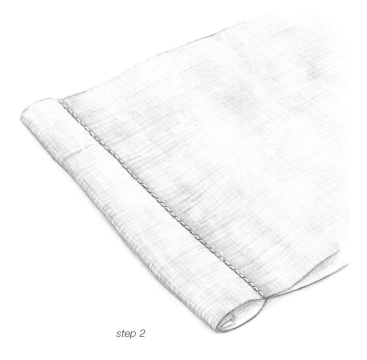

step 2

2 Join the sheer and linen fabrics using a French seam to conceal the join. Lay the pieces right sides facing and lined up where they are to join.

3 Turn in the sides 1cm and press. Then turn in a further 1cm, press, tack and machine down. Turn up the bottom 1.25cm and press. Then turn up a further 1.25cm and press. For a mitred corner, open out and fold the corner in at 45-degree angle and press. Open this out and cut back the fabric to the fold mark of the triangle. Fold the two creases back up. Pin, tack and machine down.

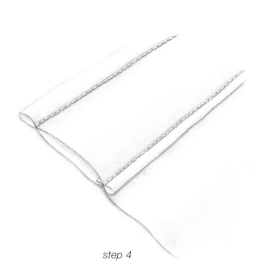

step 4

4 For the top, fold down the sheer 1.25cm and press. Fold down a further 6.5cm and press. Using tailor's chalk and a ruler, draw two lines one 1.25cm and the other 4.5cm from the top. Machine along the two lines to form the pocket.

step 5

5 Portiere rods are useful in many circumstances: dormer and casement windows, over doors as draught excluders and even on windows where there is limited room. Once the portiere rod is fixed in place, slip the pocket of the curtain panel over the arm.

semi-sheer curtain panels   71

simple swag

The practical and decorative uses of a simple swag are many: the drape of the fabric can soften the hard lines of an austere window, add colour and texture, hide ugly roller blind fixings or add height to a window. This strong yellow linen is edged with a charming gingham ribbon.

simple swag

Materials

Wooden batten

Fabric

Sewing thread

Ribbon for edge

Contrast fabric for ties

Strong cotton thread

It is best to use a loosely woven fabric, such as linen, raw silk or soft muslin, as this will have better draping qualities than other textiles. Putting in the folds can be somewhat awkward, but a little perseverance usually pays off.

1 Cut a piece of batten to slightly wider than the frame of the window and cover all over with the same fabric as the swag, using a staple gun to fix in place. Attach this batten just over the top of the window. Cut a piece of the fabric the width of the window plus about 50.75cm either side for the tails to hang down, by a drop of about 112cm.

3 For the ties, cut two strips of the contrast fabric 20cm long by 11.5cm wide. Fold in half lengthwise with right sides facing and press. Machine around two long and one short side 1.25cm from the edges. Turn right side out. Fold in the remaining raw edges 1.25cm and machine closed. Press.

step 2

2 Turn in both ends 1cm twice to make a double hem. Press, pin, tack and machine down. Do the same for one of the long edges. For the remaining raw edge, turn up a 1cm hem and press. Over this pin a length of the ribbon to cover the raw edges, pin, tack and machine down.

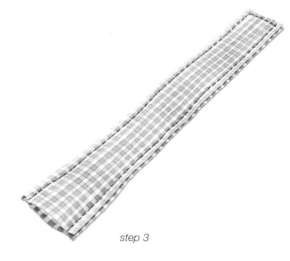

step 3

4 To fix the swag, find the centre of it and, using a staple gun, staple it straight onto the top of the fabric-covered battening. Continue stapling out to each corner. Gather the loose fabric into folds at one end, making a series of neat pleats at the side. Secure this using strong cotton thread tied in a knot. Fold the other side in the same way. Wrap the ties over the gathered ends and secure with a couple of staples.

step 4

unlined roman blind

The clean lines of a Roman blind work well in both traditional and contemporary interiors. Roman blinds are unfussy and require only a minimum of fabric. This deeply pleated, unlined blind is made from thin linen to which a monogram has been embroidered. It filters the light to give a soft effect.

unlined roman blind

Materials

Wooden batten

Length of antique
linen with neat
selvedges

Touch-and-close tape
cut to the width of
the window

3 x screw eyes

Sewing thread

6 x blind rings

3 x thin wooden
dowels width of blind

Cleat

Blind cord

The narrow red lines along the selvedges of this antique linen looked so smart that I decided to incorporate them into the blind. If you can't find anything similar and need to add a hem to each side, turn in both sides of the fabric 1.25cm twice, press and machine.

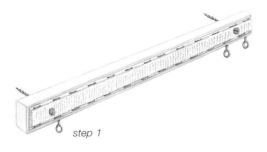

step 1

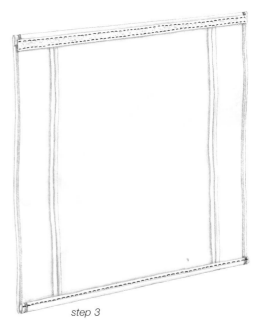

step 3

1 Cut a wooden batten the width of the window and cover with fabric, using a staple gun. Staple the hook side of the piece of touch-and-close tape to the front of the batten. Attach two screw eyes to the bottom of the batten, 15cm from each side, and one on the same end you intend to put the cleat. Attach the batten to the frame of the window.

2 If the fabric width is the same as the window, so much the better. If not, add widths to either side, incorporating the woven selvedges (in this case the red edge of the linen), so you end up with a piece of linen the width required plus 11.5cm for dowels and 2.5cm for hems.

3 For the top, turn down the linen 1.25cm and press. Machine the fluffy side of the touch-and-close tape to cover the raw edge. For the bottom hem turn up 1.25cm and press. Then turn up a further 1.25cm. Press, tack and machine down.

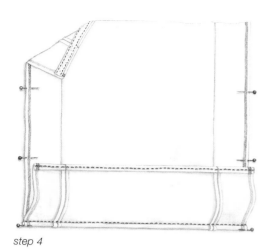

step 4

4 With the panel right side up, divide it into four equal sections and mark with pins. This is where the three pleats will be made. Fold up the linen at the first pins and press. Using tailor's chalk and a metal ruler draw a line 2cm from the fold. Machine along this line to form the first pocket. Repeat for the other two pockets. Sew two blind rings onto the back of each pleat 15cm in from the sides. Insert the dowels into the pockets.

step 5

5 Fix the cleat to the side of the window. To string the blind, cut two lengths of blind cord three times the drop of the blind. Working on the back of the blind and starting with the vertical row that is the farthest from the cleat side, knot the cord to the bottom ring using a double knot. String the cord through the two other rings. Repeat for the other side. Now attach the blind to the fabric-covered batten. Run the blind cord through the screw eyes so that they meet on the cleat side. Pull the two cords to pull up the pleats and ensure they are straight by adjusting the cord. Tie into a knot at the end and attach to the cleat.

lined roman blind

Instead of the more usual vertical stripes used in window treatments, try a horizontal stripe for a change. With the pleats of the blind, it makes a widow look wider and rather elegant.

lined roman blind

Materials

Wooden batten

Fabric for blind

Touch-and-close tape
cut to the width of the
window

4 x screw eyes

Antique monogram

Sewing thread

Cotton lining fabric,
such as cotton
gingham

9 x blind rings

4 x thin wooden
dowels

Cleat

Blind cord

The technique for this lined Roman blind is very similar to the unlined version. The main difference is that here the pockets are at the front and the blind is lined with contrasting red gingham, which looks fresh and inviting from the street, too!

1 Prepare a fabric-covered wooden batten as in step 1 of the Unlined Roman Blind (see page 78), but add a third screw eye in the middle for extra support.

step 2

step 3

2 Cut a piece of both the fabric and the lining to the drop required plus 15cm (for 4 dowels) and 2.5cm seam allowance, by the width required plus 2.5cm seam allowance on both sides. Cut out the monogram. Turn under 0.5cm all round and press. Place the fabrics right sides together and pin, tack, then machine 1.25cm in from the two sides and bottom. Turn right side out and press.

3 Lay blind right side down, turn down the top 1.25cm and press. Pin the fluffy side of the touch-and-close tape to the top of the fabric. Tack and machine down.

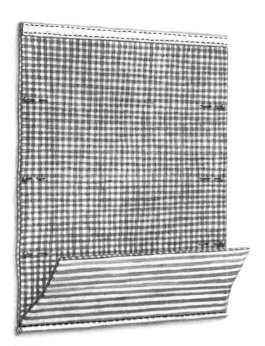

step 4

4 With the right side facing down, divide the length of the blind into five equal sections, and mark each side with pins. Fold up the linen at the first set of pins and press. Using tailor's chalk and a metal ruler draw a line 2cm from the crease and machine down to create a pocket. Repeat for the rest of the pockets. These pockets are at the front of the blind, so with the blind still right side down, sew three rows of rings to the back of each pleat, 15cm from each side and one in the middle. Insert the dowels into the pockets. Pin the monogram to the blind and using small slip stitches, hand sew to the front fabric only. Follow the instructions for stringing the blind as in Unlined Roman Blind (see page 79).

adding a monogram

Old linens often yield monograms that can be cut out as patches and appliquéd to the front of curtains and blinds, either by hand, using embroidery thread and blanket stitch, or with an overlocker on the sewing machine. Hand embroidering a monogram is also special; use embroidery thread and work it in cross stitch or back stitch.

swedish roll-up blind

Used for centuries all over Sweden, blinds like this one are easy to make and easy to use. Traditionally they are made from a single layer of woven linen that is reversible, as you can see the back when they are rolled up. The glass rings let the cord glide through smoothly for opening and closing. This blind is backed in simple gingham to provide a contrast to the floral fabric.

swedish roll-up blind

Materials

Fabric for front, such as lightweight cotton

Contrast fabric for back

Sewing thread

1.25cm wooden dowel 0.5cm narrower than width of blind, ends covered in the fabric

Wooden batten 0.5cm narrower than blind, covered in same fabric as back of blind

2 x glass rings

Blind cord

Cleat

It is better to use two fabrics of the same weight for this blind, so it will glide smoothly. The fabrics need to be perfectly aligned and pressed to prevent any wrinkling once the blind is up.

1 Cut a piece each of the two fabrics the width of the blind plus 2cm by the drop required plus 9cm. Cut two pieces of the fabric for the front panel 23cm long by 7.5cm wide for the ties. Place the large front and back pieces edge to edge and right sides facing. Pin, tack and machine the two sides and the bottom, 1cm from the edges. Turn right side out and press. Now topstitch the blind by machining down very close to the edge on the two sides and bottom. Tack the wooden dowel to the bottom of the front of the blind to hold in place.

step 2

2 For the ties to hold the glass rings, fold a strip in half lengthways, right sides facing and press. Pin, tack and machine 0.5cm from the edges on the long side. Turn right side out and press.

3 Staple the top of the blind to the back of the batten. Fold the ties in half and slip through a glass ring on each, then staple the raw edges to the back of the batten, about 17.75cm from each side. Cut two lengths of blind cord about three times the drop of the blind. Knot one end of one cord and staple to the back of the batten in the centre of the tie. Repeat for the other. Attach the cleat. Put up the batten, being careful to use a bradawl to make holes in the fabric covering the batten so as not to twist it. Roll up the blind to the

step 1

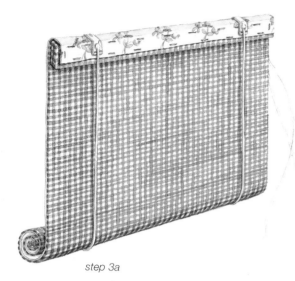

step 3a

front, enclosing the dowel, and bring round the first piece of cord and thread it through the glass ring above it. Repeat for the other cord. Thread the cord furthest away from the cleat end through the next glass ring. Pull the cords gently until the blind rolls up easily and knot off.

step 3b

matching fabrics

When teaming two patterns, remember that one must always be a foil for the other. A floral print almost always looks good when teamed with a check or a stripe that picks up one of the colours. Neither the colour nor the scale of the foil should overwhelm the colour and pattern of the floral. If in doubt, most patterns look great backed with a plain white or cream linen.

bedlinen

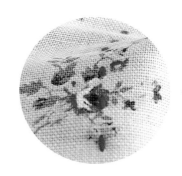

lace-edged coverlet

With all the gorgeous double cloth and mattelasse fabrics now on the market, let alone the array of vintage textiles, you can easily transform a bed with a custom-made coverlet. Rummaging in antique markets for a length of vintage lace or old silk ribbon can provide the inspiration for endless sewing ideas.

lace-edged coverlet

Materials

Matelasse cotton
fabric

Antique cotton lace

Sewing thread

Velvet ribbon

By washing and preshrinking all the components of this bedspread, it will not only look elegant but also be practical. The lace is machined to the mattelasse fabric and the velvet ribbon is neatly hand sewn to hide the machine stitches.

1 Cut a piece of matelasse cotton fabric to the size required plus an extra 2cm seam allowance all the way around. (Join widths if necessary.) Cut a length of lace long enough to go all the way round the outside edge of the matelasse cotton, plus 2.5cm for each corner to pleat. With the matelasse cotton facing right side down, turn in both long sides 2cm and press, pin and tack. Repeat for the two shorter sides. Pin the lace right side down and facing out over the folded edges, making a small pleat at each corner. Tack and stitch down to incorporate the turned-in seams.

step 2

2 Cut a length of velvet ribbon slightly longer than the perimeter of the bedspread. Using tiny slip stitches, hand sew both edges of the ribbon to cover the join of the lace and the matelasse cotton, mitring the corners.

step 1

choosing fabrics

The best way to narrow your search for fabric is to choose a good texture and
look for colours that will suit the room or simply for colours that you love. This can
include anything from a vintage quilt to the most high-tech double-woven cloth.
Choose trimmings to enhance the fabric, pulling out a colour, introducing a new
texture or creating a pattern (see Ribbon-decorated Coverlet on page 94).

ribbon-decorated coverlet

Matelasse cotton
fabric

A selection of ribbons
and tapes

Sewing thread

The simplest quilted cotton bedspread can be totally transformed by adding randomly spaced strips of assorted ribbon. Suddenly, there is a sophisticated and modern feel to the bedspread, which is achieved with great ease and very little expense.

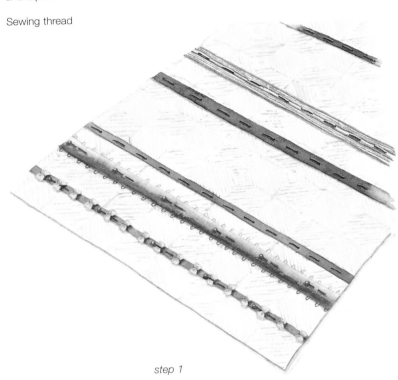

step 1

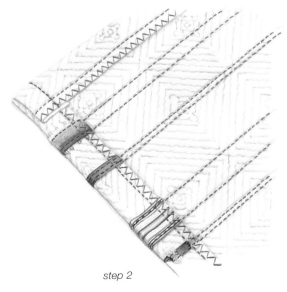

2 Zigzag stitch all the way around the perimeter of the matelasse cotton to prevent fraying, catching in the ends of the ribbon. Lay the cotton right side down and turn in both long sides 5cm, press, tack and stitch. Repeat for the two shorter sides, keeping the corners crisp and neat.

step 2

1 Cut a piece of matelasse cotton fabric to the size required plus an extra 5cm seam allowance all the way around. (Join widths if necessary.) Cut lengths of the various ribbons and tapes to the same as the width as the matelasse cotton. Lay the matelasse cotton right side up and pin the ribbons and tapes across the width of the bedspread to form random stripes. Tack, then stitch each one down along both sides to secure.

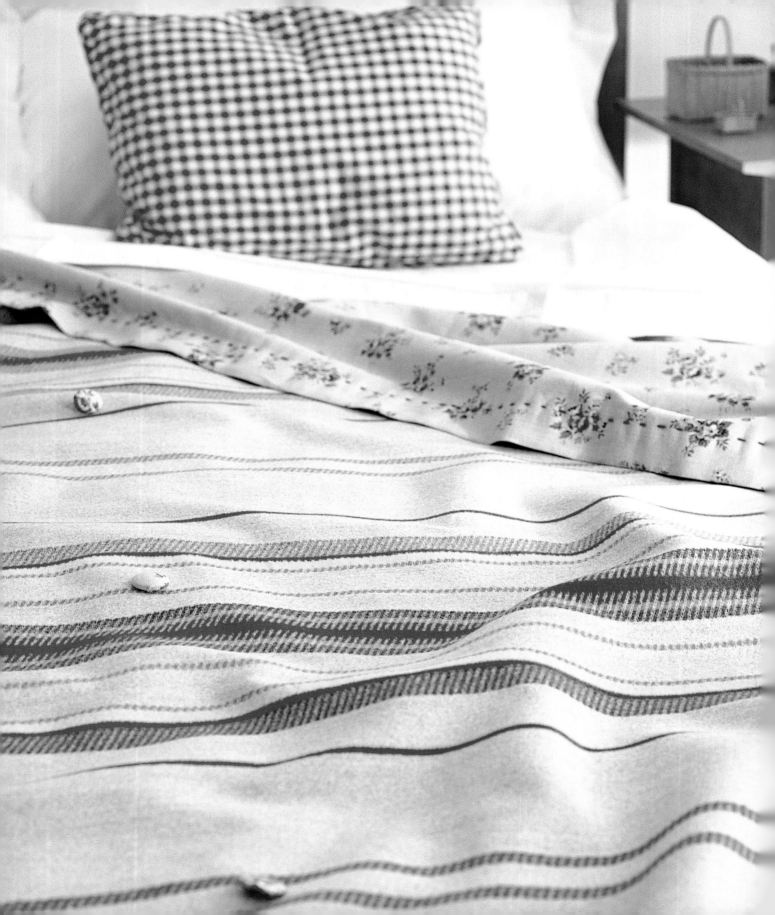

cotton-backed
wool bedspread

Lightweight wool, backed with a fresh summery linen print, gives this bedspread a dual life: the warmth of the wool looks cosy for the winter months, whilst for summer you can use the reverse side in cool linen for a crisper style. The hand-stitched border gives the bedspread a bespoke look that is easy to achieve.

cotton-backed wool bedspread

Wool fabric

Linen fabric

Embroidery cotton

Button covering kit for 6 buttons

6 x small shirt button for back

Sewing thread

To prevent the two fabrics from sliding about, they are anchored at regular intervals with covered buttons on one side and small shirt buttons on the other. Use a chunky embroidery cotton for the hand-stitched border and make sure the colour visually enhances or ties together both fabrics.

1 Cut a piece of wool to the size required. Cut a piece of linen to the same size as the wool plus an extra 6.5cm all the way around for the turnover. Turn in 2cm on both long sides of the linen and press. Turn in 2cm on the other two sides of the linen and press. Turn in a further 4.5cm on both long sides of the linen and press. Turn in 2cm on other two sides of the linen and press. Open out the second folds and place the wool into the creases, right side up.

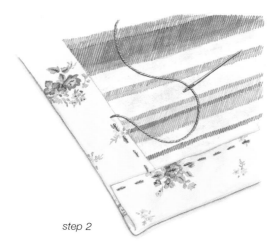

step 2

2 Bring over the folded edges, pin and tack. Using embroidery cotton, secure the two fabrics together with running stitch all the way around.

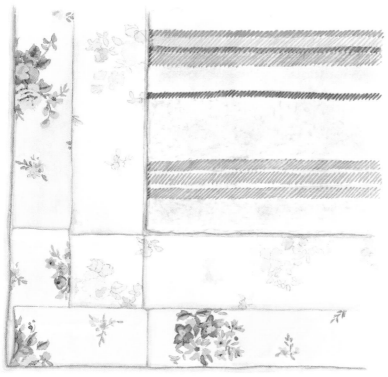

step 1

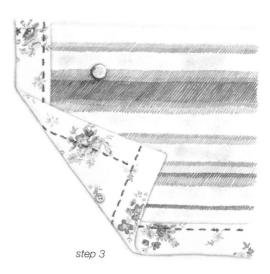

step 3

3 Cover six buttons with the linen following the kit manufacturer's instructions. Position the buttons evenly on the wool side of the bedspread and pin into place. Sew on each button, attaching it to a shirt button on the floral side to anchor it.

fleece throw with pompoms

Materials

Thick fleece

Tapestry wool

Thick cardboard

Sewing thread

This fun fleece throw with big woollen pompoms adds a touch of joy and flair to any bedroom. The contrasting blanketstitched edges give a tailored finish to the fleece. This project would make a wonderful wedding present.

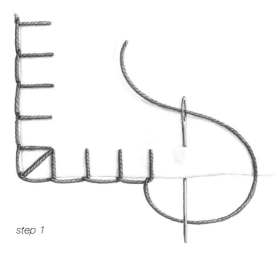

step 1

step 2

1 Cut the fleece to the size required. Using the tapestry wool, sew large blanket stitches evenly all the way around the perimeter of the fleece.

2 To make the pompoms, cut two circles about 10cm in diameter from the cardboard. Into each cardboard circle, cut another circle about 4.5cm in diameter to form a ring. Cut a 15cm length of wool for tying the pompom later and insert it between the cardboard rings, avoiding the central hole. With the two cardboard rings together, wrap the wool around the rings until they are covered by two thicknesses of wool all the way around. Slip a pair of scissors between the cardboard rings and snip the wool all the way round. Tighten the tying wool around the pompom and carefully remove it from the rings. Tie the tying wool to secure. Make several pompoms in this way and hand stitch them to the top of the fleece.

ruffle-edged eiderdown

There is a lovely nostalgic English country house look to an eiderdown. The combination of a flowery chintz, backed with a rough linen gingham, and the puffy thickness of the squares give this cover a warm, wintry feeling. It is still possible to find well-worn old eiderdowns in antique markets but having one's favourite fabrics and colours adds a special touch.

ruffle-edged eiderdown

Making this eiderdown yourself requires some sewing experience. Keeping together all the various layers and squares is quite fiddly, but well worth persevering. There are some companies that will make them for you. Use goose down fillers (see pages 184–87 for suppliers) for the ultimate in eiderdown luxury!

1 Cut a piece of the cotton fabric for the top to the size required adding 6.5cm all around for each square (allowance for the quilting), plus an extra 2cm seam allowance all the way round. Cut a piece of the cotton fabric for the bottom and several layers of wadding to the same size. (Join widths if necessary.) Cut 12cm-wide strips of the cotton fabric for the ruffle and join to make one long strip twice the perimeter of the eiderdown.

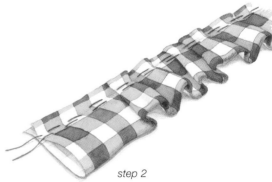

step 2

2 Fold the ruffle in half lengthwise with right sides out and press. Sew two rows of running stitch 1.5cm from the raw edge. Pull the threads at each end to make even gathers until the frill is the same length as the perimeter of the eiderdown.

step 3

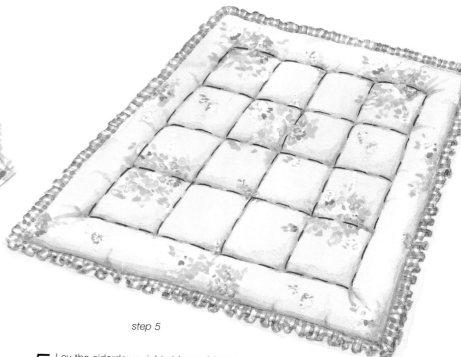

step 5

3 Lay the backing fabric right side up and place the ruffle around the perimeter, 0.5cm in from the outside edge and aligning raw edges. Pin, tack and stitch 2cm in from the outside edge. Turn backing fabric over and press ruffle to the outside.

5 Lay the eiderdown right side up. Measure and mark out an outside border. Measure and mark out equal intervals along this outline to make a grid of squares. Pin, tack and stitch.

Materials

Cotton fabric, such as glazed cotton chintz, for the top

Cotton fabric, such as gingham, for bottom and frill

Enough wadding to make three or four layers

Sewing thread

step 4

step 6

4 Turn under and press 2cm all the way around the cotton fabric for the top. Tack. Lay the backing fabric right side down and place several layers of wadding on top, followed by the cotton fabric for the top. Pin and tack layers together all the way around close to each edge.

6 To finish, hand stitch the top fabric to the ruffle using tiny slip stitches.

patchwork throw

If you, like many people, hoard scraps of leftover fabric, or like me, collect antique textiles, this is the perfect solution for their practical use. Theme them by colour, texture or pattern and transform them into an heirloom quilt. This one, which is trimmed with a rich navy cotton velvet, was made for my god-daughter's 21st birthday.

patchwork throw

Materials

Mixture of coloured
linens and cottons,
old and new

Sewing thread

Velvet for edging

Lining fabric for
backing (for a double
bed you will need
200cm fabric, 150cm
wide)

This bedspread was made using mainly antique textiles, with just a few new ones thrown in. It is important that all that patches are prewashed to prevent any future shrinkage. It also helps if the weight and weave of the patches are similar – mixing a loosely woven linen with a tightly woven cotton will create distortion.

1 Cut out enough fabric patches of the same length but varying widths to make the size of throw required. Lay the patches out randomly in strips to give an idea of how the finished throw will look.

2 Starting with the first row, pin, then tack the patches together with 1cm seam allowance. Stitch. Press seams out flat. Repeat for each subsequent row. Pin, then tack the strips of patches together also with 1cm seam allowance. Stitch. Press seams out flat.

step 3

3 For the edging, cut strips of velvet on the cross, 5cm wide. With right sides together, stitch with 1cm seams to make a continuous length.

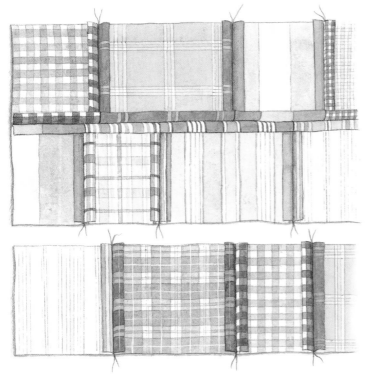

step 2

step 4

4 With right sides together, lay the velvet strip around the edge of the patchwork throw with raw sides edge to edge. Pin and tack into place, pleating the velvet at the corners. Stitch 1cm from the edge.

step 5

5 Bring the velvet edging round to the reverse side of the throw, turning under 1cm. Pin and hand sew into place. Cut the lining fabric to the size of the throw adding 1cm seam allowance all the way around. Turn under 1cm, press and hand sew lining to the throw.

choosing fabrics

For any patchwork project the most important factor is to make sure all the patches, be they old or new or a combination, are similar weights and types of fabric. Mixing a wool with a thin cotton creates tension and cleaning problems, so stick with compatible textiles. Always pre-wash and iron patches before sewing, so that any shrinkage can happen at this stage.

cot quilt with embroidered initial

The softness of an antique linen makes a tactile and cossetting quilt, which is suitable for a baby or toddler. A patchwork of assorted linen scraps forms the basis for this quilt, which is then oversewn with a contrasting herringbone stitch. The edges are hand sewn with a simple running stitch in the same embroidery thread. To personalise the quilt, hand embroider one of the patches with an initial.

cot quilt with embroidered initial

Materials

35 x 18cm squares of
antique linen scraps

Sewing thread

Two shades of
lavender embroidery
cotton

Cream linen for
backing

The design of this tempting little cot quilt is so simple that you need only the most
rudimentary of sewing skills. The charm of this piece is in the embroidery and the
mixture of antique cream and ivory linens.

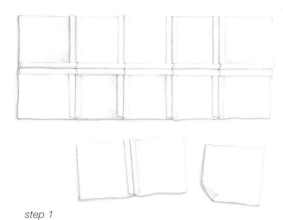

step 1

1 Lay out the linen patches into seven rows of five squares. Starting with the top row, pin, then tack the squares together with a 1cm seam allowance. Stitch. Press seams out flat. Repeat for each row. Pin, then tack the strips of sewn squares together also with a 1cm seam allowance. Stitch. Press seams out flat.

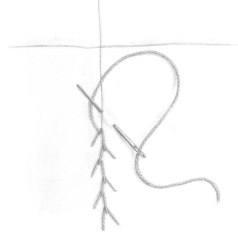

step 2

2 Using the embroidery cotton, work vertical rows of large feather stitches. Embroider the horizontal rows with the same stitch until all the patchwork seams are concealed. Using the darker thread, embroider a large initial onto one square.

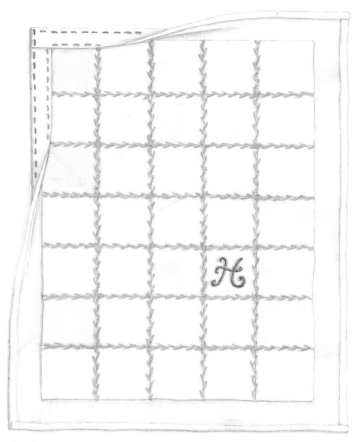

step 3

3 Cut a large piece of linen the same size as the patchwork plus an extra 10cm all the way around for the border. Lay the linen backing right side down, turn in 1.5cm on the two longer sides and press. Turn in 1.5cm on the other two sides and press. Place the patchwork on the linen backing, making sure it is centred. Fold in the two long sides to just cover the patchwork edges. Pin and tack in place. Fold in the top and bottom in the same way. Pin and tack. Using embroidery cotton, work a row of running stitches around the inside and outside edges of the border to secure the patchwork. Press.

tailored bedlinen

Admittedly, there is a plethora of bed linen on the market, but sometimes the perfect thing is just elusive: the colour is wrong or the texture is too rough. The very fine handkerchief linen used for this duvet cover with its matching pillowcases is of the very highest quality, so it will last for years and years. The simple shapes are trimmed with rickrack.

duvet cover and pillowcases

Materials

Extra wide linen or cotton

Rickrack

Sewing thread

Snap fasteners

Many textile companies now offer extra wide fabrics, which are perfect for making bedlinen. This finely woven ivory linen was prewashed to prevent future shrinking. You could substitute most other trimmings for the rickrack, as long as they are colourfast.

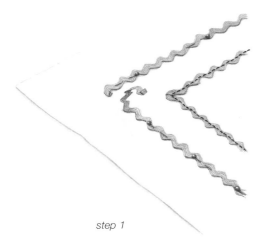

step 1

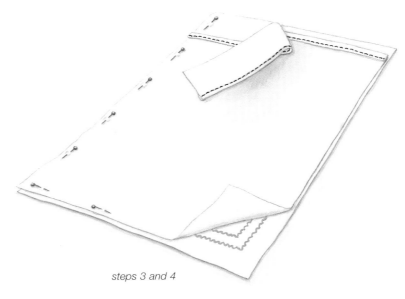

steps 3 and 4

1 Cut two pieces of linen or cotton to the width and length of the duvet plus an extra 1.5cm seam allowance all the way around. Cut a piece of linen or cotton to the width of the duvet plus 2.5cm by 20cm for the envelope closure. Cut two lengths of rickrack to the size of the top panel. Pin, tack and stitch the rickrack to the top panel, turning under the two raw edges of the rickrack where they meet.

step 2

2 Take the short piece of fabric for the envelope closure and turn down a double 1.5cm hem. Press, pin, tack and stitch. Take the back panel of the duvet cover and, with the right side down, turn down 2.5cm twice to make a hem, along the width of it. Pin, tack and stitch.

3 Lay the top panel with the rickrack, right side up and lay the back piece, right side down, aligning the three raw edges. The hemmed edge will come slightly short of the piece trimmed with rickrack (by 5cm). Pin and tack 1.5cm from the three raw edges.

4 Keeping the two layers right sides together, lay the short piece over the envelope end, aligning the raw edges and with the hemmed seam right side up. Pin, tack and stitch 1.5cm from the edge, around the four sides of the duvet cover. Turn right side out. Attach snap fasteners along both edges of the opening. Press.

matching pillowcases

For the pillowcase with the edge of the rickrack peeping out, follow the instructions for the Simple Cushion on page 12 and adding the rickrack as shown on page 15. Alter the size to suit.

For the pillowcase with the rickrack running down two sides, follow the instructions for the Simple Cushion, but before going to step 2, pin, tack and stitch the two strips of rickrack to the front piece of the pillowcase, on the right side. Proceed to step 2.

tailored bed valance

This bed valance requires some sewing experience, as a good degree of accuracy is needed for the very tailored finish. For a less-experienced sewer it would be easier to make this using a plain fabric, so the pattern doesn't need lining up.

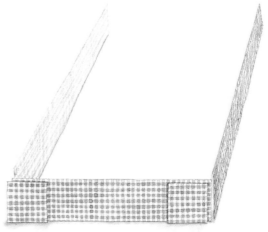

step 1

1 The valance skirt is made from five pieces of fabric. Cut two side panels of cotton to the length of the bed plus 15cm. Cut an end panel of cotton to the width of the bed base plus 30cm. Add 3cm seam allowance to the length. Cut two pieces of cotton for the pleats, each 30cm long and equal to the height of the side and end panels.

2 For the central panel, cut a piece of lining fabric to the length and width of the bed less 30cm. Cut two 19cm wide strips of the cotton fabric and the same length as the bed plus 5cm and two strips 19cm wide and equal to the width of the bed plus 5cm.

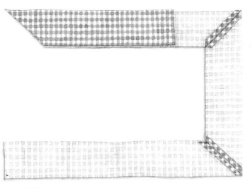

step 3

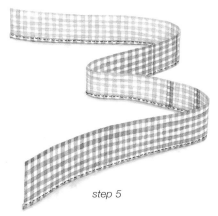

step 5

step 4

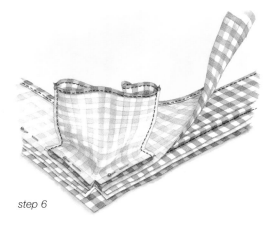

step 6

Materials

Medium-weight cotton, such as gingham

Sewing thread

Thin piping cord

Lining fabric

3 For the central panel, with right sides facing, place a long strip and a short strip together with raw edges aligning. Pin and tack together at a 45-degree angle, diagonally from the top corner. Machine down, stopping 1.5cm from bottom edge of strip. Attach other strips in the same way until you have a frame. Cut back excess fabric at joins to leave 1.5cm seams and press open. Then press in a 1.5cm fold to the wrong side all around inside edge of border.

4 Place the central lining panel right side up and lay the frame over it, right side up, making sure it overlaps evenly. Pin, tack and machine the border to the central panel. At the top end of the panel (the headboard end) press in a double 1.5cm hem.

5 Take the three pieces of fabric for the skirt and the two pieces for the inverted pleats, and with the right sides together, join one side of each corner pleat to a side panel, then the other side of each corner pleat to the end panel. Pin, tack and machine. Turn up a double 0.5cm hem at the bottom and press. Pin, tack and machine down.

6 Cover a length of piping cord with fabric so it is long enough to go round the two sides and end of the bed. Place the central panel right side up and pin the piping around the three unhemmed sides, raw edges together. Place the skirt over the central panel, right side down, raw edges facing out and align the pleats at the corners. Pin, tack and then machine together 1.5cm from the edges, keeping the piping cord to the inside of the stitching. Press.

tablelinen

scallop-edged tablecloth

The fresh, crisp quality of gingham is hard to beat in looks, practicality and price. Make a cloth to fit your dining or picnic table and add a decorative scalloped edge. Team the tablecloth with some gingham napkins finished with a velvet ribbon or rickrack border to complete the look.

scallop-edged tablecloth

The secret to the success of this tablecloth is in working out the scallops really accurately, especially at the corners. Adjust your template to suit and remember that the corner scallops could be a little bigger if it helps with the measurements.

Materials

Lightweight cotton fabric, such as gingham

Lining fabric

Cardboard for template

Sewing thread

step 1

1 Cut a piece of cotton to the length and width required plus 2.5cm seam allowance. Cut a rectangular piece of the lining to the same measurements as the cotton. Measure 12cm in from the outside edges of the lining fabric and cut out, leaving just a rectangular frame. Make a template for the scallops using the cardboard and a round object, such as a cup or small plate, as a guide. Draw a three-quarter circle at one end of the template for corners of the tablecloth. Trace the outline of the scallops with a marker pen and cut out the cardboard template.

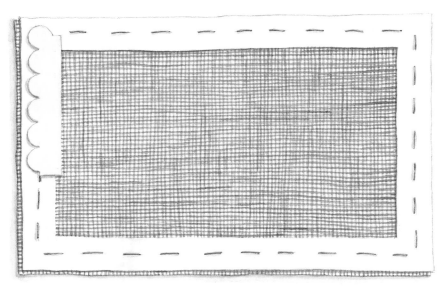

step 2

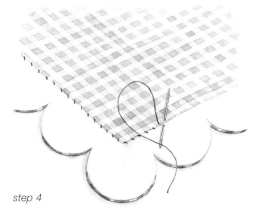

step 4

2 With the right sides together, pin and tack the band of lining fabric to the outside edges of the cotton. Using the cardboard template and tailor's chalk, trace the outline of the scallops 1.5cm in from the outside edges.

4 Turn the scallop border right side out and press. Handstitch the lining to the wrong side of the cotton to hold in place.

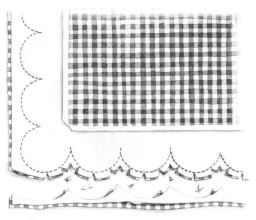

step 3

3 Stitch around each scallop along the trace line. Trim back the excess fabric around each scallop to 1.5cm and make snips every 5cm so that the fabric lies flat. Clip the inside corners of the lining fabric to 1.5cm. Remove the tacking stitches, fold back and press.

Materials

Lightweight cotton fabric, such as gingham

Velvet ribbon or rickrack

Sewing thread

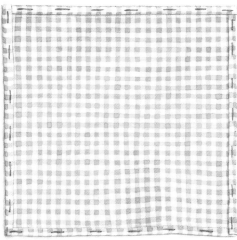

step 1

1 Cut a piece of cotton to 50cm square. With the fabric right side up, turn in to the front 0.5cm all round, press and tack.

2 Cut a length of ribbon to 205cm. Starting at one corner and with outside edges aligning, pin the ribbon to the edge of the hemmed napkin. Mitre each corner by making small folds and tucking them under. Cut the two raw ends at 45-degree angles and fold under to form another mitre on the final corner. Tack, then machine down both outside edges of the ribbon.

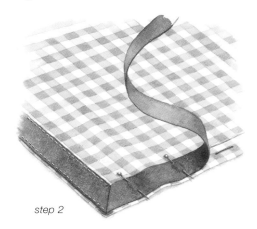

step 2

denim place mats

Add a splash of fun colour to your table at the same time as protecting the surface from hot plates or food and wine stains. Sturdy denim is practical and tightly woven so there is little fraying and it now comes in many colours. Contrasting bias binding and embroidery thread add a little zip to the denim.

denim place mats

If you can, use a thin domette for the interlining of these place mats so that the bias binding can easily incorporate the layers. For heavier pots and casseroles, use a thicker interlining and a wider bias binding.

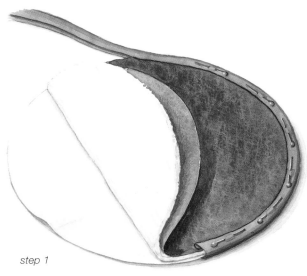

step 1

1 Cut circles of the denim, domette and lining. Tack the three layers together keeping the domette in the middle. Pin the bias binding around the circumference, sandwiching the three layers and tack in place.

2 Using embroidery cotton, sew small running stitches around the outside edge to secure the bias binding over the three layers. Again using running stitch, embroider the place mats either in concentric circles or spirals.

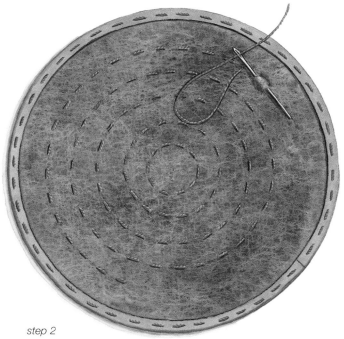

step 2

Materials

Denim

Thin domette

Lining

Ready-made bias binding

Sewing thread

Embroidery cotton

monogrammed picnic rug

There are so many wonderful mould- and waterproof fabrics on the market now, that we no longer need the dark, plastic-backed blankets of our childhood. Make your own personalised picnic rug with a monogram and large rickrack edging to add a little style and amusement to outdoor dining.

monogrammed picnic rug

Add a monogram to the front of the rug or, if you prefer, a flower or any other favourite motif. I have also made a smaller picnic rug for my dog and added a large bone motif to the centre!

1 Cut a piece of both the wool and the backing fabric to the size required plus an extra 2cm seam allowance. Cut a length of the rickrack to the perimeter of the rug. Cut an extra piece of the backing fabric large enough for the monogram.

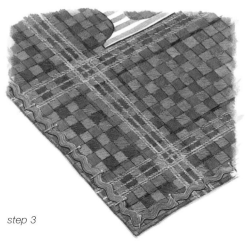

step 3

Materials

Wool for front, such as tartan

Waterproof fabric for backing

Paper template for monogram

Embroidery cotton

Large rickrack braid

Sewing thread

step 2

2 Lay the paper template for the monogram over the right side of the small piece of backing fabric, making certain it is on the straight grain and trace the outline with tailor's chalk. Cut out the monogram. Lay this over the centre of the wool tartan, right sides up, pin and tack. Using blanket stitch and embroidery cotton, sew the monogram to the front of the wool.

3 With the wool front right side up, lay the rickrack along the outside edge, pin and tack. Stitch along the centre of the rickrack.

step 4

4 Lay the piece of backing fabric over the wool front, right side down, and pin. Tack together exactly along the centre of the rickrack (you will have to keep lifting the top layer to guide you). Leave an opening of about 40cm along one side. Stitch along tacking line. Turn right side out and press. Close the opening using neat slip stitches.

fitted tablecloth with box pleats

Disguise an old or unattractive side table with a fitted box-pleated cloth, edged in luxurious velvet ribbon. Give the cloth a glamorous look with a fairly long skirt, but don't take it right to the floor – an instant dust collector. The cotton ticking I've used here is durable and washable, as are cotton velvets.

fitted tablecloth with box pleats

The deep box pleats give this skirt a flounced and fun look. Lining up the stripes requires a little planning, so it might be easier for less-experienced sewers to use a narrow stripe or a plain fabric.

1 Cut a piece of the cotton fabric to the size of the tabletop plus an extra 2cm seam allowance all the way around. Cut a strip to measure three times the perimeter of the table by the drop required and add 2cm seam allowance all the way around. (Join pieces for the length if necessary.) Cut a piece of the velvet piping to the perimeter of the table plus an extra 2cm. Cut a piece of the velvet ribbon to three times the perimeter of the table plus an extra 4cm.

step 2

2 Lay the cotton for the top panel right side up. Align the raw edges of the velvet piping 2cm from the edges of the panel, making right angles at the corners. Tack in place.

Materials

Heavyweight cotton
fabric, such as ticking

Velvet piping

Velvet ribbon

Sewing thread

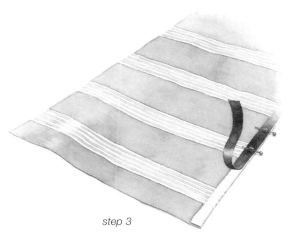

step 3

the centre panel and one at each corner. Divide the perimeter of the panel by the number of pleats to give the distance between pleats. Pin the top edge to secure each pleat, folding the excess fabric to the back to make the pleat. Check the skirt fits the centre panel. Pin the other end of each pleat and press. Tack along the top edge and machine 2cm from the edge.

step 6

3 Lay the long strip of cotton for the skirt right side up and turn up one long side 0.5cm and press. Lay the velvet ribbon along this fold to cover. Pin, tack and then stitch.

4 Join the two short ends of the skirt 2cm from each edge, open out the seam and press flat.

step 5

6 To assemble the tablecloth, lay the top panel with the velvet piping right side up. With raw edges aligning, place the skirt right side down along the edges of the top panel. Carefully pin the skirt so that the stitched lines are together and the velvet piping is snug between the layers. Tack, then machine stitch using the piping foot of the machine to sew as closely as possible to the piping. Snip the corners and trim back any excess fabric. To prevent fraying, zigzag the raw edges. Turn right side out and press.

5 Decide on the number of pleats, making sure there are an equal number of opposite sides of

organandie tablecloth with napkins

There is something very special and festive about crisp, white linen organandie. Here, it is teamed with giant gold polka dots that work equally well for a traditional Christmas lunch as for a special summer wedding party.

organdie tablecloth with napkins

The polka dots are hand sewn to the organdie cloth and napkins in a random pattern using a lightweight gold thread. For a neat finish, the trick is to get the circles as round as possible when turning under the hem.

2 Using the cardboard template and tailor's chalk, trace out as many circles onto the gold fabric as required. Cut out. Pin the circles to the right side of the cloth in a random polka dot pattern. Turn under the perimeter of each circle as little as possible, press and tack into position.

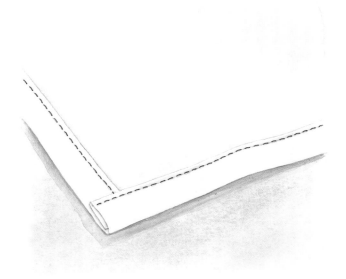

step 1

1 Cut the organdie to the size required plus and extra 10cm all the way around. Turn under both ends 5cm twice, press and tack. Turn in both sides in the same way, keeping the corners neat. Stitch close to the edge of the folds.

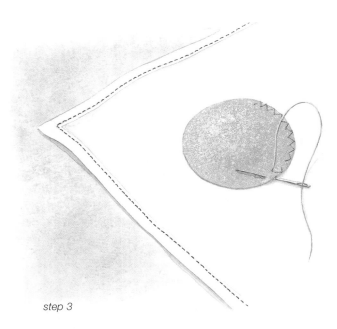

step 3

3 Using the gold embroidery cotton, hand sew each circle in place with zigzag stitches. Make the napkins in the same way but scale everything down, including the size of the polka dots.

Materials

Lightweight fine linen organdie

Sewing thread

Cardboard template of circle, 0.5cm larger than required

Gold fabric

Gold embroidery cotton

lampshade skirt with ties

These special decorative skirts sit over card lampshades to give them an instant lift. Brilliant white organdie works well and would look lovely in a bedroom or dressing room.

lampshade skirt with ties

Materials

Paper for template

Fabric, such as
lightweight cotton or
organdie

Sewing thread

Instead of organdie, use crisp cotton tea towels for a different look. Alternatively, find a lightweight fabric that enhances the colours of your room scheme. Don't use a heavy fabric as it won't drape or look pert like these skirts do.

step 1

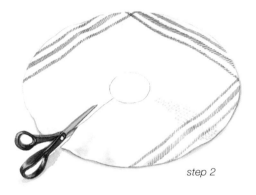

step 2

2 Pin the template to a piece of fabric and outline with tailor's chalk. Cut out the fabric, then cut a straight line between the outer and inner circumferences.

1 Make a paper template of the card shade that is to be covered. Do this by measuring the diameter of the top and drawing a circle with this diameter plus 5cm in the centre of the paper. Measure the height of the shade and draw a line from the central circle out by that measurement adding 2.5cm. Draw another circle of that diameter. Cut out the card template.

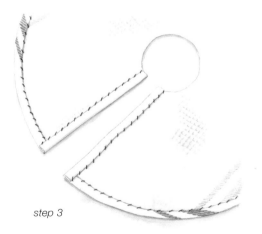

step 3

3 Turn under a double 0.5cm hem, press and slip stitch by hand. Do the same along the two straight edges, making neat right-angled folds at the corners.

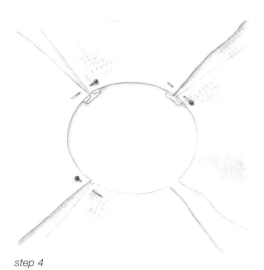

step 4

4 Turn the fabric right side up and make three small box pleats around the inner circle, making each inverted pleat about 0.5cm. Pin and tack. The inner circle should now have just a slightly larger diameter than the top of the lampshade.

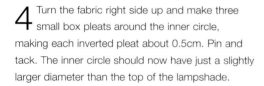

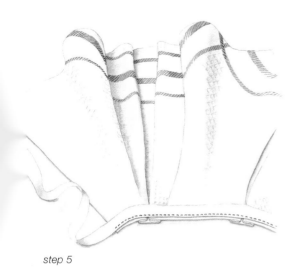

step 5

5 Cut a strip of the fabric, on the bias, the diameter of the inner circle plus 46cm, by 2cm. With right sides together, centre the strip along the top edge of the skirt. Pin and tack 0.5cm below the raw edge. Machine the strip in place 0.5cm from the edge.

6 Turn the strip over the top raw edge of the skirt to hide the machine stitching and fold under 0.5cm. Pin and slip stitch by hand. Fold in the raw edges of the tails and slip stitch them together by hand. Press.

seating

padded chair cushion

Create a little cushioned comfort for an antique or plain wooden chair. The cushion is shaped to the contours of the chair seat and then attached to the chair back with tailored button-on fabric tabs.

padded chair cushion

Materials

Paper for template

Piece of upholstery
foam (4cm thick)

Fabric, such as
medium-weight
cotton or linen

Old linen for the
bottom of chair
cushion

Sewing thread

4 buttons

Use a sturdy fabric for this chair cushion as it will take a lot of wear and tear. The antique linen I have used for the bottom of the cushion and the insides of the tabs adds a smart dressmaker's touch.

1 Make a template of the chair seat by placing the paper over the seat and tracing its outline, taking care when tracing around the struts. If necessary, tape the paper in place and snip around the struts.

2 Pin the template to the foam and trace the outline using tailor's chalk. Remove the template and cut out the foam. Lay the same template over a piece of the main fabric and trace the outline using tailor's chalk. Remove the template and cut out adding a 1cm seam allowance all the way around. Repeat with the old linen for the bottom of the chair cushion.

3 For the side panel, cut a strip of the fabric to the perimeter by the thickness of the foam adding a 1cm hem allowance all the way around. Join the two short ends with a 1cm seam, stitch and press the seam open.

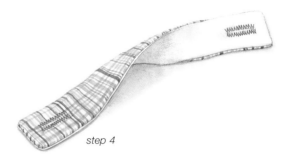

step 4

4 For the ties, cut two strips from both the main fabric and the linen to the length required adding a 1cm seam allowance by 3.5cm wide. Lay a strip of the fabric and a strip of the linen right sides together. Pin and tack along both long sides and one short side 1cm from the edge. Stitch. Turn right side out and press. Fold in the raw edges of the open end. Use small, neat slip stitches to close the opening. Make a buttonhole on both ends of each tie (see page 37).

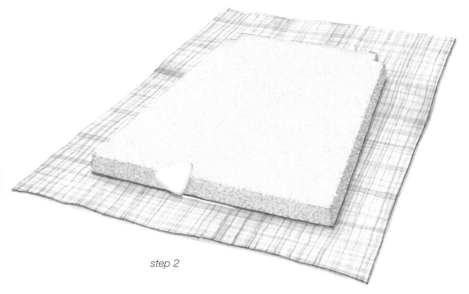

step 2

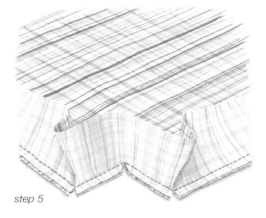

step 5

5 With right sides facing and starting at the centre back, pin the side panel to the top panel, taking care to pin it right into the corners. Start stitching 5cm from the end of the side panel at the centre back, 1cm from the raw edges. When you get to within 5cm of the centre back again, adjust the side panel to fit the rest of the back edge and stitch a 1cm seam in the side panel. Open the seam out and press. Stitch the rest of the side panel to the top panel. Clip the seam allowance around the corners.

adding a zip

To make the cover removable and easier to wash, you could insert a zip into the bottom of the cushion. Cut two pieces of fabric for the bottom panel and follow the instructions given for inserting a zip in the Ruffle-edged Cushion on page 18.

6 Attach the bottom panel to the side panel in the same manner, leaving an opening for the foam. Turn right side out. Press. Sew buttons to the side panel on both sides of two back corners. Insert the foam. Use small, neat slip stitches to close the opening. Button on the ties around the chair struts to secure the cushion in place.

chair cover with ruffle

It's hard to beat the look of a rich, crisp white linen for fresh appeal. Here it is teamed with sharp red and white ribbon for a snappy yet classic look. A well-fitted chair cover has the same allure as a couture outfit, something special and lasting – yet in this case relatively simple to make. Because it is a loose cover, it can easily be removed for laundering.

chair cover with ruffle

As your chair is unlikely to be exactly the same shape as the one shown here, you will have to adapt the design to fit. Just remember to make a paper template to ensure a snug fit or, if in doubt, make up a rough sample in cheap muslin or cotton to try out before cutting into an expensive fabric.

Materials

Lining fabric for template

Lightweight woven linen

Sewing thread

Striped grosgrain ribbon for edging and ties

1 Using the lining fabric, make a template of the chair seat, including the top surface and depth of the seat. Marking where the chair struts join the back of the seat.

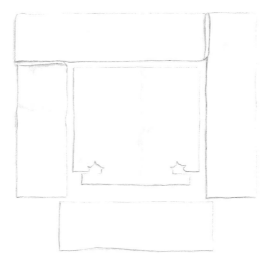

steps 2 and 3

2 Lay the seat template over the linen. Pin, then cut out the centre panel adding 1cm seam allowance all the way around. Zigzag all raw edges to prevent the linen fraying. Cut tiny snips around the position of the chair struts, turn in a tiny hem and hand sew to neaten. Machine darts on the two front corners to fit the seat.

3 Cut a strip of linen, about 20cm deep, approximately the length of the front and two sides of the chair seat but adding an extra 30cm for gathering. (Join the fabric if necessary.) Cut another strip of linen, again about 20cm deep, the length of the back but adding an extra 10cm extra for gathering. Zigzag one long and two short edges of both strips.

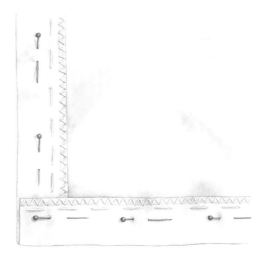

step 4

4 For the front and side skirt, lay the strip of linen right side down. Turn and stitch 1cm hems along both short sides. Press. Turn and stitch 1cm hem along the bottom edge. Press.

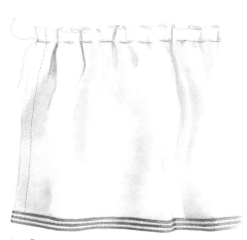

step 5

5 Cut a piece of ribbon long enough to run along the bottom edge of the front and side skirt, adding an extra 1cm. With the front and side skirt right side up, pin and tack the ribbon to the pressed hem, turning 0.5cm to the back on both side ends. Stitch ribbon in place taking care to sew only on areas that match the sewing thread. Using strong thread, sew running stitch along the top edge of the front and side skirt, 1cm from the edge, leaving long threads at either end. Pull up the threads to make gathers in the skirt to fit the front and sides of the centre panel.

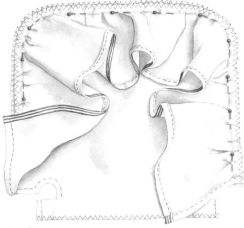

step 6

6 With right sides together, lay the gathered skirt around the seat top with raw sides edge to edge. Pin and tack the skirt to the seat. Stitch 1cm from the edge. Repeat steps 4–6 for the back skirt. Turn right side out. Press.

7 Cut four pieces of ribbon for the ties. Hand stitch the ribbon to both sides of the back corners. Tie the ribbons around the struts of the chair to secure the cover.

chair cover with box pleats

Materials

Paper for template

Fabric, such as floral
cotton

Lining fabric

Sewing thread

Even though this is the same chair as shown in the previous project, the cover
looks quite different with box pleats made up in a pretty pink floral toile de Jouy.
You can really transform the look of a chair just by using different fabrics.

1 Make a template of the chair seat by placing the
paper over the seat and tracing its outline, taking
care when tracing around the struts. If necessary,
tape the paper in place and snip around the struts.
Pin this template to a piece of the fabric and trace
the outline using tailor's chalk. Remove the template
and cut out the chair cover seat adding a 1cm seam
allowance all the way around. Cut a piece of the
lining fabric to the same size using the template.

step 2

2 Place the fabric and lining right sides together.
Pin, tack and stitch with 1cm seam allowance
but leaving an opening at the front of the seat cover.
Turn right side out, slipstitch the opening together
and press.

3 For the ties, cut four pieces of the fabric 30cm
long by 7.5cm. Fold in half lengthwise, with right
sides facing and press. Then stitch along the open
long side and one short end with 1cm seam
allowance. Turn right side out using a pencil or
knitting needle and press. Use small, neat slip
stitches to close the opening.

4 For the front and side skirt, cut a piece of the
fabric 25cm deep by three times the length of
the front and two sides adding a 1cm seam
allowance all the way around. For the back panel
cut a piece of the fabric 25cm deep by three times
the width of the back adding a 1cm seam allowance
all the way around.

5 For the front and side skirt, turn in both short
ends 1cm and press. Stitch. Turn up the
bottom hem 1cm and press. Stitch. Repeat this for
the back skirt.

step 6

6 To make the inverted box pleats, follow the instructions in step 5 for Fitted Tablecloth with Box Pleats on page 139.

step 7

7 With right sides together, lay the pleated front and side skirt around the chair cover seat with raw sides edge to edge. Pin, tack and stitch with 1cm seam allowance. Repeat for the pleated back skirt. Hand sew the ties to the corners.

tufted bench cushion

A pretty metal bench needs the comfort of a padded seat cushion and this smart black and white checked fabric gives it a real lift. The piped edges give the cushion some rigidity and shape while the wool tufts add style and formality.

tufted bench cushion

Once you have mastered the boxed cushion, you can use the same technique to make window seats, sofa cushions or floor cushions. The secret is in accurate measuring and lining up any pattern, especially at the front edge of the cushion.

1 Cut two pieces of the fabric to the size of the required cushion adding a 3cm seam allowance all the way around (2cm of this will be taken up by shrinkage when the tufts go in). For the side panel, cut a strip of the fabric to the perimeter of the cushion adding 2.5cm by the width required. (Join pieces if necessary.)

step 2a

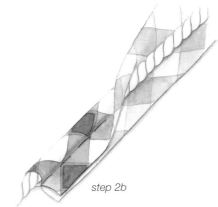

step 2b

2 To make the casing for the piping cord, cut pieces of the fabric on the bias 4cm wide. Join the pieces and press the seam flat. Place the piping cord in the centre and wrap the cord in the fabric, wrong sides facing. Tack to enclose the cord without catching it with the stitches. Stitch, using a piping or zipper foot. Make enough piping to go twice around the perimeter of the cushion.

Materials

Fabric, such as
medium-weight
cotton or linen

Piping cord

Sewing thread

Wadding

Wool or cotton tufts

Flat buttons

step 3

3 Pin the piping cord to the right side of the top panel with the raw sides edge to edge, 1.5cm from the edge. Tack in place. Pin the side panel over this, right side down, and tack, making sure to avoid sewing into the cord. Machine together as close as possible to the piping cord.

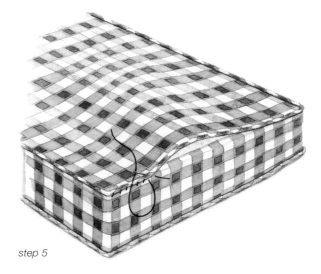

step 5

5 Insert the wadding carefully. Hand sew the opening with neat slip stitches to close.

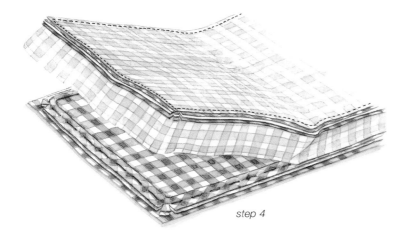

step 4

4 Pin another length of the piping to the right side of the bottom panel, with raw sides edge to edge. Tack as close as possible to the piping. Carefully lay the top and side panels over this and tack together close to the edge of the piping, leaving an opening at one end for inserting the wadding. Stitch.

step 6

6 Mark out the spacings for the tufts with pins. Attach a tuft on the top panel by sewing right through the wadding to the back and through a button. Secure the other tufts in the same way. The buttons act as anchors for the tufts and help to create the padded effect.

tailored dining chair cover

Smarten up an upholstered dining chair with a fitted loose cover. The gently shaped scallops soften the hem as well as adding elegance. Loose covers are so much more practical on dining chairs as they can be whipped off for laundering in a flash.

tailored dining chair cover

Materials

Fabric

Lining

Paper for template

Sewing thread

The hardest part of this project is achieving a pleasing scalloped pattern to suit the chair. Experiment with paper templates and hold them to the front and sides of the chair to see if your design will work, especially at the corners.

1 Cut a piece of fabric to the width plus twice the depth of the inside back of the chair, by the height plus the depth of the inside back, adding a 1.5cm seam allowance all the way around. Cut a piece of fabric the width by the height of the chair outside back, adding a 1.5cm seam allowance all the way around. For the seat top, cut a piece of fabric the width by the depth of the seat adding a 1.5cm seam allowance all the way around. For the skirts, cut four pieces of fabric and of lining to the maximum drop required by the widths for the front, the back and each side, adding a 1.5cm seam allowance all around. The width of each side panel must extend to the back edge of the back leg.

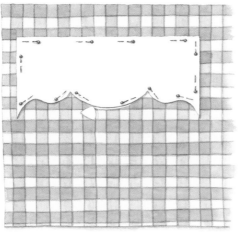

step 2

2 If the sides, front and back of the seat are the same width, make one template by cutting a piece of paper to the width and drop required, and drawing a shallow scallop pattern. Cut out and pin

to wrong side of aside panel. Using tailor's chalk, trace the outline onto the fabric. Cut out, adding a 1.5cm seam allowance all around. Repeat for the other panels and the lining. (If the sides are different widths, make a template for each one.)

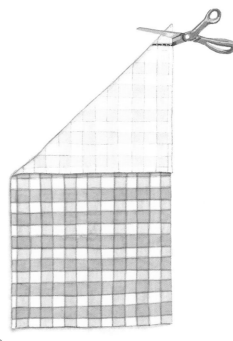

step 3

3 For the inside back panel, take the larger piece of fabric and, with right sides facing, fold the top to make a 45-degree angle. Mark the depth of the chair back across the top corner and tack a straight line to form a triangle. Stitch and cut away the excess fabric. Repeat for the other side to complete the second fitted dart for the inside back.

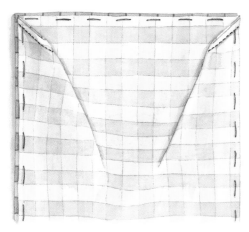

step 4

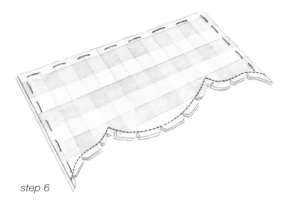

step 6

4 Lay the outside back panel right side up and place the darted inside back panel over the top, right side down, and align all raw edges. Pin and tack 1.5cm from the raw edges. Stitch the sides and top only, snipping the corners.

6 For the skirts, take one piece of the fabric and one piece of the lining and lay right sides together. Pin and tack. Machine together along the shaped edge, 0.5cm from the edge. Cut away the excess fabric and snip every 5cm. Remove the tacking. Turn right side out and press. Repeat for all the panels.

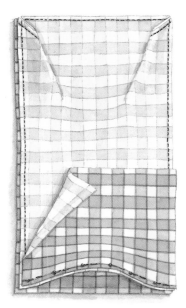

step 5

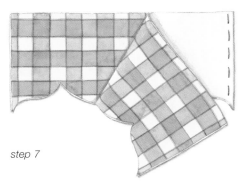

step 7

5 With right sides together, attach the seat top to the inside back panel, aligning the raw edges. Pin and tack 1.5cm from edge. Stitch together.

7 Join the four panels together by laying two panels right sides facing, pinning and tacking 1.5cm from short ends. Stitch, open out seams and press. Repeat to join all the panels like a frame.

8 To attach the skirts to the top, pin, right sides together, aligning the raw edges to the front and sides of the seat panel and the bottom edge of the outside back panel, leaving 1.5cm seam allowances all the way around.

tailored dining chair cover   167

dining chair cover with ruffle

Although this is the same chair as in the previous project, a very different effect has been achieved by using a floral fabric and richly coloured velvet to make a softly gathered skirt, which combine to give the chair a romantic and pretty feel.

Materials

Fabric

Sewing thread

Velvet ribbon

1 Cut a piece of fabric to the width plus twice the depth of the inside back of the chair, by the height plus the depth of the inside back, adding a 1.5cm seam allowance all the way around. Cut a piece of fabric the width, plus 20cm for an inverted pleat, by the height of the chair outside back, adding a 1.5cm seam allowance all the way around. For the seat top, cut a piece of fabric the width and depth of the seat adding a 1.5cm seam allowance all the way around. For the gathered skirt cut a piece of fabric four times the perimeter of the chair seat by the drop required, adding a 1.5cm seam allownce all the way around. Join pieces where necessary.

2 For the inside back panel, take the larger piece of fabric and, with right sides facing, fold the top to make a 45-degree angle. Mark the depth of the chair back across the top corner and tack a straight line to form a triangle. Stitch and cut away the excess fabric. Repeat for the other side to complete the second fitted dart for the inside back.

step 2

step 3

3 For the outside back, form the inverted pleat down the centre and pin, then tack 1.5cm from the top edge. With right sides facing, join the inside and outside back by aligning the raw edges, pinning and tacking 1.5cm from edge around both sides and top the only. Machine. With right sides together, attach the seat top to the inside back panel, aligning the raw edges. Pin and tack 1.5cm from edge. Stitch together.

step 4

4 For the skirt, stitch the two short ends together. Open out the seam and press. Turn up the bottom hem right sides facing to just less than the width of the ribbon, pin and tack. Cut a length of the velvet ribbon to the perimeter of the skirt. Pin, then tack it over the hem and machine along both outer edges to secure the ribbon.

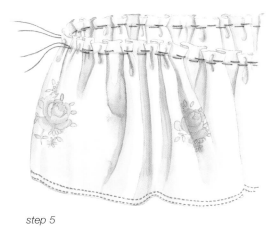

step 5

5 Sew two parallel rows of running stitch 1cm from the top edge of the skirt and gather it up evenly to measure the same as the perimeter of the seat top (including the opened out pleat). With the right sides facing, align the raw edges of the skirt with the seat top and the bottom edge of the outside back. Pin and tack together. Machine 1.5cm from the edge. Turn right side out and press. Cut three pairs of velvet ties and hand sew them to the back to close the pleat.

beaded armchair cover

Give a family heirloom a new lease of life with a gorgeous linen fitted loose cover trimmed with perky ceramic beads. On an old armchair, the fit doesn't need to be perfect. In fact, the odd gather and tuck add a casual elegance reminiscent of comfortable old country houses.

beaded armchair cover

Materials

Fabric

Sewing thread

Heavy beading on
tape

This technique takes time, but it's more than worth it when you have a smart new
cover for an old chair. Leave plenty of extra fabric in the seam allowances for any
adjusting the fabric to fit.

steps 1 and 2

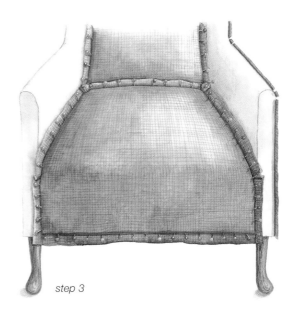

step 3

2 Cut a length of fabric for one of the outside
side panels, adding 7.5cm all the way around
for seams. Pin to the side wrong side out. When
cutting around a shaped area make small snips in
the fabric every 2.5cm to help the fabric ease
around the curves. Repeat for the other side.

1 Cut a length of the fabric for the inside back of
the chair, adding a 7.5cm seam allowance all
the way around. Using dressmaker's pins, pin the
panel, wrong side out, to the chair inside back.

3 Cut a piece of fabric for the seat, including the
drop at the front of the chair adding 7.5cm all
the way around for seams. Pin to the chair with the
fabric wrong side out.

step 4

4 Cut a piece of fabric for one of the inside side panels, adding 7.5cm all around for seams. Pin to the chair with the wrong side out. Repeat for the other side.

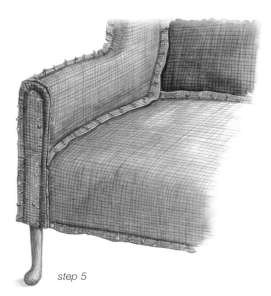

step 5

5 Cut a strip of the fabric for the front of the arms taking it from the top right down so it is level with the bottom edge of the seat. With the wrong side out, pin this to the chair and repeat for the other arm.

6 For the outside back, cut a length of the fabric, adding 7.5cm all the way around for the seams. If the back on your chair splays out at the top, cut the panel to the wider measurement all the way down to allow the cover to be pulled over the chair. Pin the panel to the back, wrong side out.

step 6

7 Trim off all excess fabric to leave a 2cm seam allowance. Remove the pins one by one and replace them with dressmaker's pins and then pin the fabric pieces together, making smooth seam lines. Once you have gone over the whole chair, carefully gather up the cover. Tack along the pinned edges. Remove the pins and stitch. Turn up the hem to the drop required, pin and tack. Pin the beading to the outside edge of the hem and stitch to incorporate the hem. Press.

simple sofa cover

A crisp, cotton loose cover in a romantic floral print brings instant summer breeziness to any sofa – an effective transformation for any worn piece of old furniture. Once you have mastered the technique, you will be hooked!

simple sofa cover

If it is your first attempt at a loose cover, it is probably best to start with a small and clean-lined sofa with few cushions. Although it is a logical process, the fewer panels you have to join together, the easier the project.

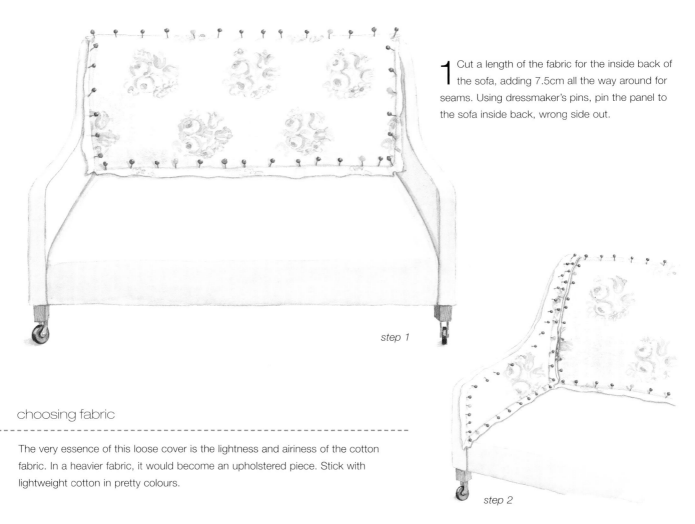

1 Cut a length of the fabric for the inside back of the sofa, adding 7.5cm all the way around for seams. Using dressmaker's pins, pin the panel to the sofa inside back, wrong side out.

step 1

step 2

choosing fabric

The very essence of this loose cover is the lightness and airiness of the cotton fabric. In a heavier fabric, it would become an upholstered piece. Stick with lightweight cotton in pretty colours.

2 Cut fabric for one of the inside arm panels, adding 7.5cm all around for seams. Pin to the sofa, wrong side out. Repeat for the other side.

Materials

Fabric

Sewing thread

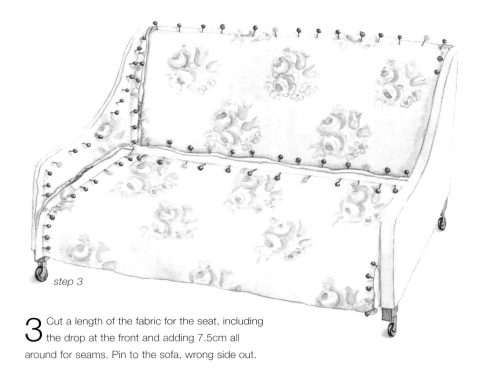

step 3

3 Cut a length of the fabric for the seat, including
the drop at the front and adding 7.5cm all
around for seams. Pin to the sofa, wrong side out.

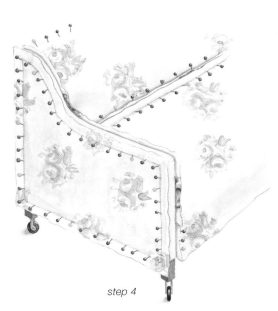

step 4

4 Cut a piece of fabric for one of the outside
arms panels, adding 7.5cm all around for
seams. Pin to the sofa, wrong side out.

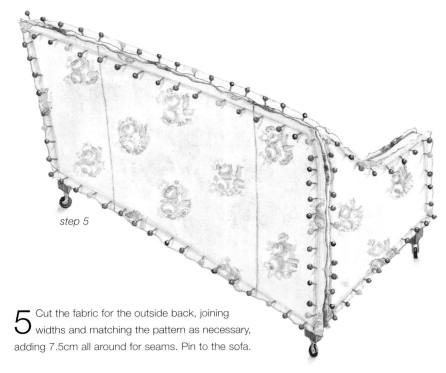

step 5

5 Cut the fabric for the outside back, joining
widths and matching the pattern as necessary,
adding 7.5cm all around for seams. Pin to the sofa.

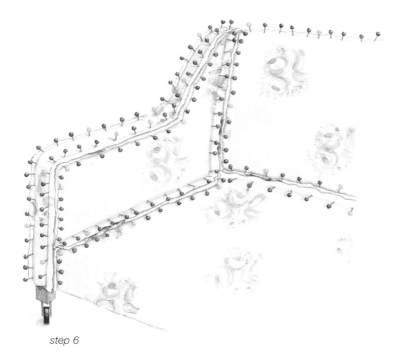

step 6

step 9

8 For each seat cushion, cut out two pieces of fabric the size of the seat cushion adding 2cm all the way around for seams. Cut a side panel from the fabric to the same length as the perimeter by the width of the cushion, adding 2cm all the way around for seams.

6 Cut a piece of fabric for panel along the top of each sofa arm, adding 7.5cm all around for seams. Pin to the arms, wrong side out.

7 Trim off all excess fabric to leave a 2cm seam allowance all the way around. Remove the pins one by one and repin the fabric pieces together, making smooth seam lines. Once you have gone over the whole sofa, carefully take the cover off. Tack along the pinned edges. Remove the pins and machine. Turn up the hem to the drop required, pin and tack. Stitch.

9 With the right sides facing, pin, then tack the side to the top panel. Stitch 2cm from the edges, snipping the corners.

10 Attach the bottom panel with the right sides facing, leaving an opening at the back for inserting the cushion pad. Turn right side out. Insert the cushion pad and hand sew the opening with small, neat hand stitches to close.

allowing for shrinkage

Loose covers inevitably take some wear and tear, so they need to be laundered. Make sure the loose cover is large enough to allow for any shrinkage. If necessary, wash a small sample of the fabric to check for shrinkage.

bean bag with handles

You will have the whole family fighting over this huge squashy bean bag – even the pets! Made in chic linen toile de Jouy and finished with velvet piping, it's the perfect place to relax. Big handles make it easy to move the bean bag around the house.

bean bag with handles

It's tempting to overfill a bean bag with beads, but this makes it uncomfortable to sit in. You will need to experiment before sewing it up, but bear in mind that the beads will compact a bit with time.

1 Cut two circles of the fabric to the desired size, adding an extra 1.5cm seam allowance all the way around. Measure the circumference of the circle and divide this by four. Then cut four panels of fabric for the sides to this measurement by the height required, adding 1.5cm seam allowance all the way around.

step 2

2 Lay one of the side panels right side up. Cut a length of the velvet piping to the height of the panel and lay over one end, aligning the raw edges. Pin, then tack into place. Using a piping or zipper foot, machine close to the piping. Then lay another panel over the top of this, right side down, and pin close to the piping, then tack. Machine down. Join all four panels in this manner.

Materials

Fabric

Velvet piping cord

Sewing thread

Sack of beads for filling

step 3

3 For each handle, cut two strips of fabric 30cm by 10cm. Fold in half lengthwise, right sides facing. Press. Machine the long sides and one short side. Turn right side out, press and close the end with small, neat slip stitches. Machine the ends of each handle to the right side of opposite panels.

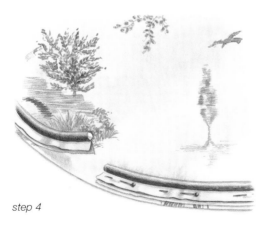

step 4

4 Lay the top panel right side up and cut a piece of the velvet piping to the circumference of the circle. With raw edges aligning, pin, then tack the piping to the outside edge, tapering the ends off into the seam allowance. Repeat for the bottom panel.

5 Lay the top panel right side up and carefully put the side panel over the top, right side down, aligning the raw edges. Pin and tack. Machine, taking care to stitch close to the velvet piping and through all the layers.

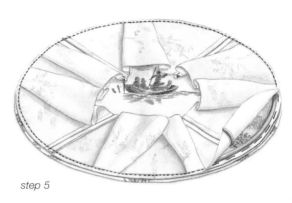

step 5

6 To attach the bottom panel, lay it right side up and carefully align the remaining raw edges of the side panel, right sides down, around the perimeter. Pin, tack and then machine together, leaving a gap for inserting the filling. Turn right side out. Fill with beads and close up using small, neat slip stitches.

suppliers

Abbott & Boyd
www.abbottandboyd.co.uk
Fabrics and trimmings

B. Brown
Tel: 08705 117118
Utility fabrics, tickings and felt

The Blue Door
74 Church Road
Barnes
London SW13 0DQ
Tel: 020 8748 9785
www.bluedoorbarnes.co.uk
Fabrics, furniture, trimmings and glass rings

Brunschwig & Fils
10 The Chambers
Chelsea Harbour Design Centre
Lots Road
London SW10 0XE
Tel: 020 7351 5797
www.brunschwig.com
Fabrics, trimmings, wallpaper, furniture

Cabbages & Roses
www.cabbagesandroses.com
Fabrics, wallpaper, accessories

Cameron Fuller
www.cameronfuller.co.uk
Curtain poles and accessories

Cath Kidston
8 Clarendon Cross
London W11 4AP
Tel: 020 7221 4000
www.cathkidston.co.uk
*Mail order and branches.
Fabrics, wallpaper, home accessories*

Chelsea Textiles
7 Walton Street
London SW3 0JD
Tel: 020 7584 0111
www.chelseatextiles.com
*Embroidered and crewel work textiles,
trimmings, accessories*

Clarence House
www.clarencehouse.com
Fabrics, wallpapers, trimmings

The Cloth Shop
www.clothshop.co.uk
Fabrics and trimmings

Cole & Son
www.cole-and-son.com
Wallpapers and fabrics

Colefax & Fowler
110 Fulham Road
London SW3 6XL
Tel: 020 7244 7427
Fabrics, wallpapers, trimmings

Cope & Timmins
Tel: 020 8803 3333
www.copes.co.uk
*Large range of tracks, poles, accesories,
haberdashery & curtainalia*

Crowson Monkwell
www.crowsonfabrics.com
Fabrics, trimmings and wallpapers

The Curtain Exchange
133 Stephendale Road
London SW6 2PG
Tel: 020 7731 8316
www.thecurtainexchange.net
*Branches nationwide. Quality secondhand
curtains*

Decorative Living
55 New Kings Road
London SW6 4SE
Tel: 020 7736 5623
Antiques and made to order furniture

De Le Cuona Designs Ltd
1 Trinity Place
Windsor
Berkshire SL4 3DE
Tel: 01753 830 301
www.delecuona.co.uk
*Handloomed linens, silks,
paisleys, wools*

Denim in Style
www.deniminstyle.com
Denims in huge range of colours

Designers Guild
267–271 Kings Road
London SW3 5EN
Tel: 020 7351 5775
www.designersguild.com
Contemporary fabrics, trimmings, wallpaper,
furniture & accessories

Eiderdown Studio
Tel: 01395 271 147
Makers of eiderdowns and other
soft furnishings

Fabrics Galore
Tel: 020 7738 9589
Large selection of affordable fabrics

The General Trading Co.
2 Symons Street
Sloane Square
London SW3 2TJ
Tel: 020 7730 0411
www.general-trading.co.uk
Furniture, linens,
household accessories

Gingham Goods
www.ginghamgoods.com
Large range of gingham and accessories

GP&J Baker
For enquiries Tel: 01494 467 467
www.gpjbaker.co.uk
Fabrics, trimmings, wallpaper

Guinevere Antiques
574 Kings Road
London SW6 2DY
Tel: 020 7736 2917
www.guinevere.co.uk
Antique linens and textiles

Highly Sprung
310 Battersea Park Road
London SW11 3BU
Tel: 020 7924 1124
www.highly-sprung.co.uk
Many branches – sofas, sofa beds & chairs

The Holding Co.
241 Kings Road
London SW3 5EL
Tel: 020 7352 1600
www.theholdingcompany.co.uk
Mail order and branches
Everything to do with storage

Ian Mankin
109 Regents Park Road
London NW1 8UR
Tel: 020 7722 0997
Mail order and branches
Fabrics, checks, stripes & plains

Jali
Apsley House
Chartham
Canterbury
Kent CT4 7HT
Tel: 01227 831 710
www.jali.co.uk
MDF radiator cover kits &
decorative fretwork

Jane Churchill
110 Fulham Road
London SW3 6RL
Tel: 020 7730 9847
Fabrics, trimmings, wallpaper, accessories

Jean Munro
www.jeanmunro.co.uk
Traditional English chintz

J.H. Porter & Son
13 Cranleigh Mews
Cabul Road
London SW11 2QL
Tel: 020 7978 5576
Bespoke metalworkers

John Lewis Department Stores
For branches call 020 7629 7711

Kerry Jupp
Tel: 01729 860246
Specialist embroiderer

Lee Jofa
www.leejofa.com
Fabrics, trimmings, wallpaper

Lewis & Wood
www.lewisandwood.co.uk
Fabrics and wallpaper

The Linen Cupboard
21/22 Great Castle Street
London W1G 0HY
Tel: 020 7629 4062
Linens, tea towels

MacCulloch & Wallis
25-26 Dering Street
London W1R 0BH
Tel: 020 7629 0311
www.macculloch-wallis.co.uk
Cottons, organdies, silks, velvets, haberdashery

McKinney & Co.
Studio P
The Old Imperial Laundry
71 Warriner Gardens
London SW11 4XW
Tel: 020 7627 5077
info@mckinney.co.uk
Bespoke curtain poles etc from glass & leather to handpainted

Malabar
31-33 The South Bank Business Centre
Ponton Road
London SW8 5BL
Tel: 020 7501 4200
Cottons, silks, crewel, and Kashmir wool

Manuel Canovas
110 Fulham Road
London SW3 6RL
Tel: 020 7244 7427
Cottons, silks, velvets and prints in large colour range

The Natural Fabric Co.
Wessex Place
127 High Street
Hungerford
Berkshire RG17 0DL
Tel: 01488 684 002
www.naturalfabriccompany.com
Calicos, cottons, linens, toiles, scrim

Nobilis Fontan
www.nobilis.fr
Fabric, trimmings and wallpaper

Nya Nordiska
2/11 Chelsea Harbour Design Centre
London SW10 0XE
Tel: 020 7351 2783
www.nya-nordiska.com
A huge range of sheers and extra wide fabrics, cottons, linens

Pavilion Antiques
Tel: 01225 866 136
A huge selection of antique linens and textiles

Pax Marie
35 Walcot Street
Bath BA1 5BN
Tel: 01225 465 130
Swedish textiles, furniture, & glass rings for Swedish blinds

Peggy Porschen
www.peggyporschen.com
Specialist cake and biscuit designer

Pierre Frey
253 Fulham Road
London SW3 6HY
Tel: 020 7376 5599
www.pierrefrey.com
Prints, cottons, velvets, weaves, trimmings

Rowan
www.knitrowan.com
Embroidery cottons and wools

The Rug Company
www.therugcompany.info
Large selection of rugs and special orders

Sahco Hesslein
24 Chelsea Harbour Design Centre
Lots Road
London SW10 0XE
Tel: 020 7352 6166
www.sahco-hesslein.com
Fabrics including modern viscose, linens and silks

Sanderson
233 Kings Road
London SW3 5EJ
Tel: 020 7351 7728
www.sanderson-uk.com
Fabrics, wallpapers, accessories

Scalamandre
www.scalamandre.com
Fabrics, wallpapers and trimmings

Shaker
www.shaker.co.uk
Furniture and accessories in Shaker style, homespun linen

Silent Gliss
01843 863 571
www.silentgliss.com
Large range of modern curtain tracks and panel systems

Tobias & the Angel
68 White Hart Lane
Barnes
London SW13 0PZ
Tel: 020 8878 8902
Antique furniture, textiles, accessories and new furniture made to order

Turnell & Gigon
Unit M20
Chelsea Harbour Design Centre
Lots Road
London SW10 0XE
Tel: 020 8971 1711
Cottons, velvets, linens, prints, trimmings

V.V. Rouleaux
54 Sloane Square
London SW1W 8AX
Tel: 020 7730 3125
www.vvrouleaux.com
Trimmings, ribbon, haberdashery

The Volga Linen Co.
Unit 1D
Eastlands Road Industrial Estate
Leiston
Suffolk IP16 4LL
Tel: 01728 635 020
www.volgalinen.co.uk
Linens, sheets, tea towels and accessories

Valerie Brooks
14b Wilcox Road
London SW4 6SP
Tel: 020 7720 0011
Bespoke curtain maker

Walcot House
Lyneham Heath Studios
Lyneham
Chipping Norton
Oxon OX7 6QQ
Tel: 01993 832 940
www.walcothouse.com
Modern metal poles, rings, tabs, ready made curtains, & eyeletting service

index

photography credits

The following companies supplied fabrics, trimmings and poles for the projects in this book.

page 12 simple cushion
cushion fabric from Brunschwig & Fils

page 14 trimmed cushions
top cushion fabric from Brunschwig & Fils, middle cushion fabric from Jane Churchill, antique trimming from Pavilion Antiques, bottom cushion gingham from Jane Churchill, antique blue linen from Pavilion Antiques, ricrac from V.V. Rouleaux

pages 16-21 ruffle-edged cushion and scallop-edged cushion
tickings from Ian Mankin

pages 22-25 bolster with silk ties
Toile de Jouy and silk from Brunschwig & Fils, rosettes and velvet ribbon from V.V. Rouleaux

page 26 gathered round cushion
fabric from Sahco Hesslein

pages 30-33 box floor cushion
stripe from Lee Jofa, antique cloth from Tobias & the Angel

pages 34-37 buttoned cushion sleeve
Toile de Jouy from Turnell & Gigon, linen from GP&J Baker

pages 38-43 decorated cushions
Fabric from Lee Jofa, trimming from V.V. Rouleaux, felt from B. Brown

pages 46-49 basic clip-on curtains
felt from B. Brown, clips from Walcot House

pages 50-53 contrast lined curtains
Cutwork fabric from Clarence House, silk from Brunschwig & Fils

pages 54-57 unlined curtains with tape ties
blue fabric from Monkwell, tape from McCulloch & Wallis

page 58 unlined curtains with sewn ties
fabric from Turnell & Gigon

page 60 lined curtains with tiebacks
cream linen from GP&J Baker, pink check from Jane Churchill

pages 64-67 ruffle-edged curtains
wool from GP&J Baker, scrim from The Natural Fabric Company, edging from Chelsea Textiles

pages 68–71 semi-sheer curtain panels
sheer from Zoffany, opaque fabric from GP&J Baker, portière kit from Cameron Fuller

pages 72-75 simple swag
yellow linen from Designers Guild, ribbon from V.V. Rouleaux

pages 76-79 unlined roman blind
linen from The Cloth Shop, monogramming by Kerry Jupp

pages 80-83 lined roman blind
stripe from Morrocan market, gingham from Fabrics Galore, monogram from Guinevere Antiques

pages 84-87 swedish roll-up blind
Floral from Colefax & Fowler, gingham from Zoffany, glass rings from The Blue Door

pages 90-92 lace-edged coverlet
Fabric from Lewis & Wood, velvet ribbon from V.V. Rouleaux, antique lace from Tobias & the Angel

page 95 ribbon-decorated coverlet
fabric from Lewis & Wood, ribbons from V.V. Rouleaux

pages 96-98 cotton-backed wool bedspread
wool fabric from Abbott & Boyd, floral linen from Cath Kidston

pages 100-101 fleece throw with pompoms
Striped wool blanket from Shaker, cream fleece from Fabrics Galore, pompoms made from Rowan Yarn, embroidered pillowcase from The Volga Linen Co.

pages 102-104 ruffle-edged eiderdown
Eiderdown made by Eiderdown Studios, floral chintz from Jean Munro, linen gingham from Gingham Goods

pages 106-109 patchwork throw
Embroidered bedlinen from Shaker

pages 114-117 tailored bedlinen
Ivory linen from Nya Nordiska, ricrac from V.V. Rouleaux

page 118 tailored bed valance
Checked fabric from Manuel Canovas

pages 122-27 scallop-edged tablecloth and napkins
Gingham scalloped cloth and velvet edged napkins from Gingham Goods

pages 128-31 denim place mats
denim from Denim in Style

page 132-34 monogrammed picnic rug
tartan from Cabbages & Roses, Sumbrella red stripe from Scalamandre, giant ricrac from V.V. Rouleaux

pages 136-38 fitted tablecloth with box pleats
Grey ticking from Ian Mankin, velvet ribbon from V.V. Rouleaux

pages 140-43 organdie tablecloth with napkins
white organdie from MacCulloch & Wallis, polka dot cookies made by Peggy Porschen Cakes

pages 150-53 padded chair cushion
blue fabric from Brunschwig & Fils

pages 158-59 chair cover with box pleats
fabric from Jane Churchill

pages 160-62 tufted bench cushion
fabric from Pierre Frey

page 165 tailored dining chair cover
fabric from Nobilis Fontan

page 169 dining chair cover with ruffle
fabric from Abbott & Boyd, velvet ribbon from V.V. Rouleaux, rug from The Rug Company

page 170 beaded armchair cover
fabric from Cole & Son, glass beading from V.V. Rouleaux

pages 175-78 simple sofa cover
fabric from Cabbages & Roses

page 181-82 beanbag with handles
fabric from Zoffany, velvet piping from V.V. Rouleaux

acknowledgements

It takes a real team to produce a book like this, and I had a great one!

My sincerest thanks go to David Montgomery, who took all the photographs for the book, with tireless enthusiasm, in wintry conditions and with little time – they are wonderful!

Melanie Williams made almost every single item for the book – she worked extraordinarily hard and her sewing is sublime. Thank you.

The artworks are exquisitely painted by Carolyn Jenkins.

Helen Lewis's art direction and quick-witted help on the photo shoots speaks for itself.

Lisa Pendreigh has been a stalwart editor; her attention to detail being of paramount importance for a sewing book.

Thank you to Jane O'Shea and Alison Cathie for asking me to do the book!